Intermediate Guide to Wood Burning

Table of Contents

Introduction.. v

Chapter 1: Introduction to Advanced Pyrography Nibs for Cutting-edge Wood Burning Art......................... 7

Chapter 2: Advanced Shading With Texturing Techniques..12

Chapter 3: Wood Burning, Colors and Much More.. 45

Chapter 4: Pyrography Easter Eggs 56

Chapter 5: Welcome Sign 65

Chapter 6: Fire Epoxy Table.................................. 75

Chapter 7: Cougar Wood Burning Project 87

Chapter 8: Pyrography Art on a Wooden Spatula 90

Chapter 9: Superhero Pyrography Portraits 96

Chapter 10: Rustic Wood Tree Ornaments............. 104

Chapter 11: Wall Art.. 109

Chapter 12: Wood Carving Board......................... 113

Chapter 13: Twig Earrings.....................................118

Chapter 14: Picture Frame 122

Chapter 15: Personalized Clothes Hangers 130

Chapter 16: Farmhouse Wooden Caddy 134

Chapter 17: Wood Burned Vases 138

Chapter 18: Wood Burned Color Block Wall Art Quote
.... 141

Chapter 19: Birthday Board 146

Chapter 20: Ceremonial Mask Pyrography Project . 156

Chapter 21: Baby Crib Mobile 171

Chapter 22: Pyrography Long Shoe Horn 175

Chapter 23: Moving on to the Advanced Level of
Wood Burning 179

References 181

Introduction

To learn intermediate wood burning, also known as the art of pyrography, you need to buy only one book, and this is the one. This book is comprehensive and discusses everything from the equipment and type of nibs to use, to the normal safety practices you should institute during your project.

You will find intermediate designs and troubleshooting tips along with an array of ideas so you can let your creativity run wild. Watch your design come to life with the use of your imagination as the embedded images emerge from the grain in an array of warm and natural colors. This *Intermediate Guide to Wood Burning* demonstrates techniques for beautiful pieces of art such as wall hangings, quote plaques, garden and tree ornaments, boat oars, and much more. While realizing your artful potential, wood burning is also a relaxing way to spend part of your day. You will learn new skills and techniques for using various tools, gain more insight into wood burning as a form of art, and learn how to express your ideas more creatively. There are so many things to love about wood burning. From the campfire smell that changes according to the wood that is used, down to the unique characteristics of each piece of wood itself, it will add to the ambiance of your work space. Natural markings such as rings and grain flow make each project different from the next.

This is an intermediate guide that quickly leads to big successes in wood burning. With the right instruments and some patience, you will be able to design unique handmade pieces of art without going bankrupt. Whether you want to design baby blocks, or customize a sign with the family name, with this craft you can create gifts and memorabilia for all of life's occasions. With the use of your wood burning tool you can create many artistic pieces from simple plaques to more advanced drawings and even portraits of your family members and pets. You can use your own freehand work, traces and other design patterns, or a combination of both. Whatever can be traced can be burned. Even if you live in a big city, crafting with wood will unite you with nature.

Chapter 1: Introduction to Advanced Pyrography Nibs for Cutting-edge Wood Burning Art

Second only to your wood burning tool, wood burning nibs are the most important necessity for this art form. They are important because they detail and create your artwork. Purchasing high quality nibs for your wood burning kit will enhance your creativeness and make the projects more enjoyable and sophisticated. There are various types of nibs used for crafting different textures and patterns with each giving their own feel to wood burning art.

The solid interchangeable nibs (universal tip) screw into the front of the burner and they are made from brass. The universal tip is used for both shading and fine line work. There are different types of nibs used for creating various wood burning patterns and textures. Each gives a different feel to a wood burned piece of art. This chapter will introduce you to different types of nibs which helps you to decide which ones are right for the projects you will be working on. It is very handy for a wood burner artist to know all about nibs.

Tips and Nibs

Ball tips have a highly shined surface and are perfectly round. the ball shape gives rise to perfectly uniform lines in any direction. Because it's surface is highly polished it is less resistant to motion giving a smoother finish.

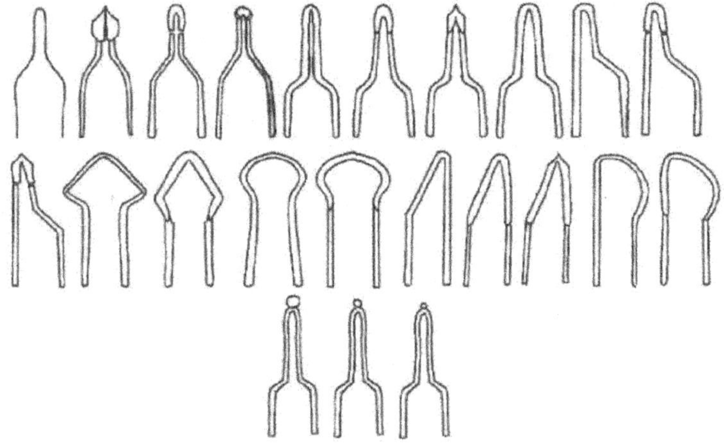

- The *flat* nib side is used to burn curving and thick lines, and for shading.

- The *blade* nib side is used to burn finer designs. (Note: if not careful, this can create very deep burns in your wood).

- Using your *fine point* or tip is generally made for creating fine lines. Using the tip and half of your blade, pull straight back in the direction of your working hand. Using no or very little

pressure keep the point at a 45 degree angle
from the wood. Remember speed (how slowly)
controls how dark or how light you want your
lines, Twirling the handle will produce curvy
lines.

- Use your *soft point* to make backgrounds,
  curves, and small circles. Keeping the pen
  parallel to the wood, think of it as floating back
  toward your working hand. Rotate your
  material so that you are always pulling back
  towards you. Let the instrument do the work
  and don't press down.

- Using a *bold point* will obviously give you a
  bold, dark line which is also slightly indented.
  Using more of the tip's side, you can apply light
  pressure, or by angling the pen a bit, you can
  create darker, bolder, wider lines. The more
  "on the side of the pen" you use the better you
  will be able to make small curves. With this
  technique do *not* twirl the pen. Do your best to
  avoid losing track of where you are burning.
  Remedy this by focusing on specific parts of
  your piece at one time. Take it slowly.

- **Ball tips** come in different sizes with the
  smaller ones being perfect for burning on small
  objects or for cursive writing. This tip glides
  over the wood making writing easier. The small
  ball nib does not have a wire running through

it, it is welded to the top. They stay hot longer than other tips and also take longer to heat up.

- ***Needle point nibs*** are used for pointillism and the very finest of lines.

- ***Mini ball tips*** are used for curved or straight lines in a compact radius. By laying it on its side flat it can be used to shade tight spaces.

- ***Skew tips*** have a slanted or angled burning tip. This tip is good for burning long lines such as those in large bird feathers.

- ***Flat skew tips*** have a blunt point and a slightly less pronounced angle. Flat skew tips are used for general wood burning.

- ***Spear tips*** have an edge that is pointed and are best used for burning in tight places and burning fine details.

- ***Round tips*** have round points. This is a good tip if you do not want to make depressions in your piece.

- ***Tight round tips*** have rounded tips that are curved but they are more narrow and smaller than round tips. Tight round tips are best for detail on flat surfaces and general wood burning.

- ***Chisel tips*** are used for shading work, long straight lines, and general detail work. They are shaped straight and flat.

- ***Round skew tips*** have a shape that is angled with a rounded end. These are fantastic for wood burn crafters who design animal carvings with detailed fur designs and bird carvings with detailed feather designs.

- ***Writing tips*** are shaped like calligraphy pens because they are curved. They can be used for fine details and for writing.

- ***Curved spear tips*** look like their name in that they are pointed and angled to one side. They aid the artist in burning sections that are hard to reach.

- ***Knife tips*** are shaped flat and sharp. They are for general use but are commonly used to burn features such as hair and feathers.

- ***Shader tips*** are flat and angle shaped so they can glide easily over the wood. They are used in a variety of shading techniques.

- ***Multi-use tips*** are very durable with a thin and curved shape. They're used for calligraphy, scaling, shading, making rippled effects, and for adding details to furs, feathers, and other life-like features.

Chapter 2:
Advanced Shading With Texturing Techniques

Just like food doesn't taste very good without spices, a picture doesn't look good without shading and textures. Most of the time the beauty is in the details, and though textures and different types of shading a pyrography art piece can look incredible. The best way to become experienced with this skill is by practicing your timing and how to gauge the temperature necessary for the shade you desire. Sitting down and putting the burner to the timber is the only way you can fully understand the best techniques for your own style of shading your artwork. When creating your wood burning art, you can get a variety of brown colors, from a very dark almost black to a super pale tan. The three techniques that control the color shade and intensity are the repetition with which you burn, the heat your pen is turned to, and your hand speed.

The heat you have your pen turned to controls how fast your wood darkens. So, the higher the heat, the darker the burn in the shortest time. Using a high heat can cause build up and make charred spots where you do not want them. The heat builds up when it is not touching the wood, so on first contact it can leave a char mark you did not intend to make. As a crafter you may pause during your burning to attend to your creative thinking and all of a sudden heat buildup leaves a dark almost black char when you start burning again. Lowering your setting can help. So, if your burner has a setting that goes up to ten, you can set your heat at three to avoid heat build up. (**Tip:** Never let the tip of your pen glow red, it can shorten the life of your instrument). Instead of a high heat setting, you can use repetition and speed to manage your color. Repeatedly burning over the same area repeatedly will build the color to your desired darkness. How many repetitions is determined by your hand speed and how high you have your heat set.

All three of these strategies, hand speed, heat setting, and repetition together control how light or dark you burn the wood. Keeping your pen set on a lower heat and using repetition and hand speed to control the darkness is essential to the quality you want to have in your art piece. Practicing with different heat levels in combination with your hand speed and repetition will help you discover what works best for you. How your tip is placed in relation to your piece can change the crispness of your edges to either blurry or sharp. Place the end of the tip of your pen with the rest of the pen angled over a section to produce sharp clean edges. Placing the tip of your pen using the entire flat end will leave softer and much thicker edges (perfect for a blurry effect). With the right positioning of your burner you can create images that appear in focus or out of focus depending on the look you want. How your pen is positioned will determine whether you achieve perfectly defined edges on a piece and guarantees that your burn will be where you intended. It is of the utmost importance that you keep the tip of your pen in the best position when you are burning near an edge where two sections or pieces touch, so there is a clear distinction between the two. The angle of your pen controls how thin of a line you can burn and how fast you can fill a section. Holding your pen at different angles controls the width of each line. The steeper the angle you burn, the thinner the line because less metal is in contact with the piece (see image below).

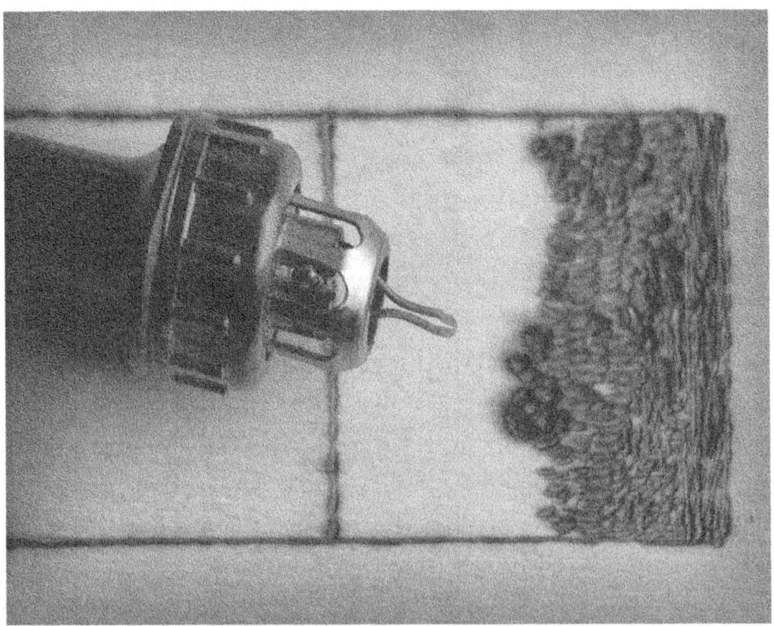

Circular Motion Shading

With a medium heat setting selected, start shading in a circular motion with constant pressure and speed. Sweep the tip over the surface of the wood in a circular pattern repeatedly until you achieve the shade you were looking for. For a lighter shade, use minimal contact between the wood and the tip. This technique gives the crafter more control over the darkness of the burn. Because of the circular motion, the tip of the pen does not spend time sitting in one place on the wood and making it too dark. Burning with a circular motion also provides a variety of textures as well as creating transitions of the levels of darkness. Burning small circles or using a circular motion will transition levels of darkness, gradually decreasing or increasing your levels because no lines are created. It will produce very soft gradients.

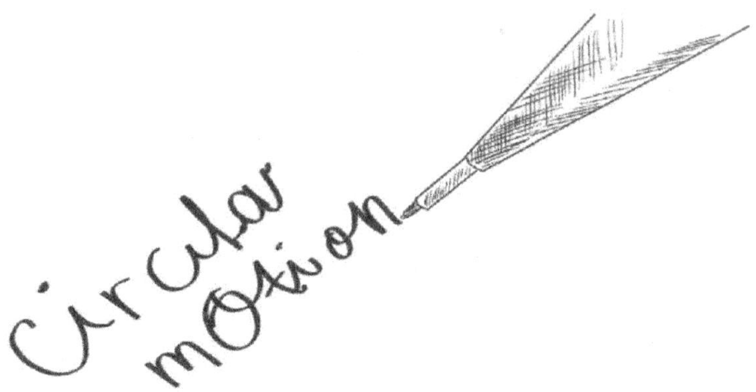

Burn a base color on your piece, burning with circular motion strokes on one end of your piece.

Continue to burn over using circular motion with each re-burn along the top. By doing this repeatedly, the color will build at the top and gradually get lighter as you move toward the bottom. Various textures can be achieved using the circular motion technique, because using this motion has a tendency to make a little textured appearance that is not solid in color. You can have a subtle texture or a very bold texture as seen in the image below.

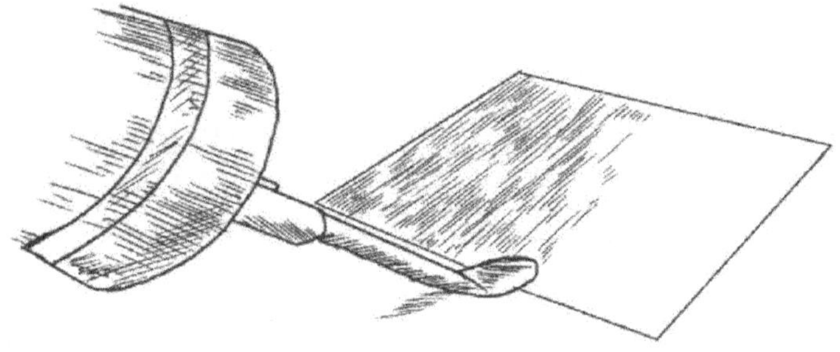

As seen in the image of the dragon below, most of the textures are created using a circular motion, varying the contrast with different colors that do not match. This example shows you how many different contrasts can be achieved as well as different textures. The contrasting colors and textures are created by changing your hand speed for different darkness levels and reburing some areas several times to create different textures. By burning in a circular motion you can see the tonal depth created to contour the dragon's body while giving a 3D appearance to its face. The background texture which looks out of focus was created using a circular motion giving the large area roundish flames with soft edges. Using a circular motion and drawing some squiggly lines produces the flame like appearance with varying brown hues of only a few shades from dark brown, to dark tan, to light brown. Using the same method as for the flames a light tan and dark brown mix was used to enhance the dragon's body and head. For the deep textured look several layers of circular motion was applied giving the appearance of crevasses burned very darkly around the dragon making it look like the dragon is coming out of the clouds. Each individual deep and dark area gets a circular motion for several layers.

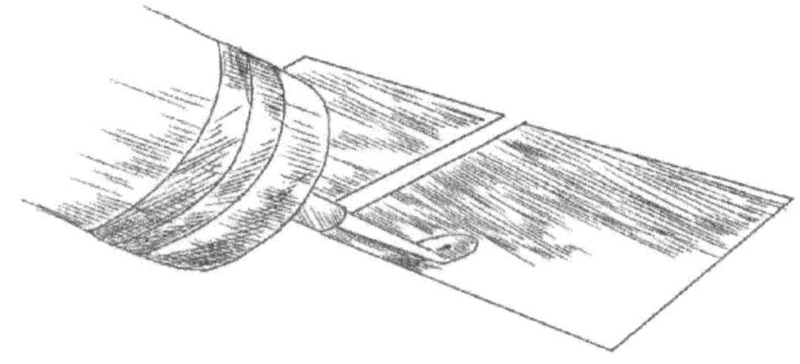

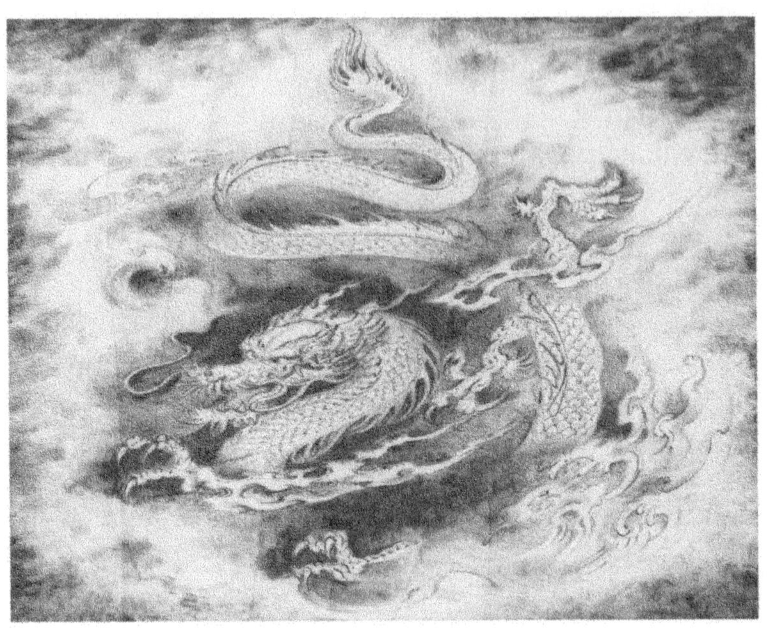

Uniform Strokes

For a surface with a smooth appearance and a solid color with no texture, you burn wide bands of color applying the same amount of pressure with the same heat level at the same speed. You start with a slow and controlled burn with the second stroke just overlapping the first stroke. Continue this process burning next to the previous burn with each stroke matching the burn before it. The dark sides of the ship are created with many uniform strokes (see image below). The ship's side has to be without texture and uniform in color. This is a perfect example of uniform strokes.

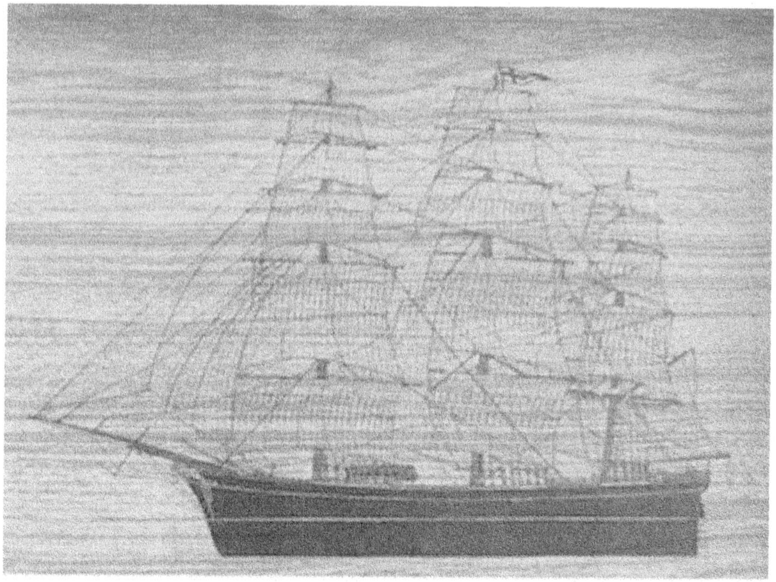

shutterstock.com • 1690173721

Pulling Motion Shading

This technique uses a one direction pulling motion. If you want your color to start very dark and end light, pull-away strokes are used. Start the stroke at the darkest end of your piece and pull your stroke in the opposite direction. The faster you stroke pulling away determines how quickly the color shades lighten. This pull-stroke technique has the benefit of providing color and contour at the same time on your piece of art. **Tip**: light areas seem closer, and dark areas seem to retreat into the background. Pulling motion shading has less control than circular motion shading as there is a greater chance of stopping in one spot and leaving a darker color there. But, for larger areas or areas with only one tone it is faster. It is important to pay attention to your wood's grain as it will be more difficult to have a consistent tone if you go against the grain. Poplar is a good type of wood for this technique. Start with a medium setting (3) and increase it as you go along. Do it slowly with a wide nib. This technique is used by pulling towards a direction without repeating your strokes. It must be done carefully or it will create dart patches. Start by placing your pen on one side and pull it to the other end or the area you intend to shade (See image A below). The pulling stroke is usually started at the edge of the wood and then the tip is carefully pulled toward you but away from the edge and lifted up at the end of the stroke. Rotate the wood rather than changing your position. Burning flower petals are often created with the pulling technique because the petal will have a curved and ruffled shape (See image B below).

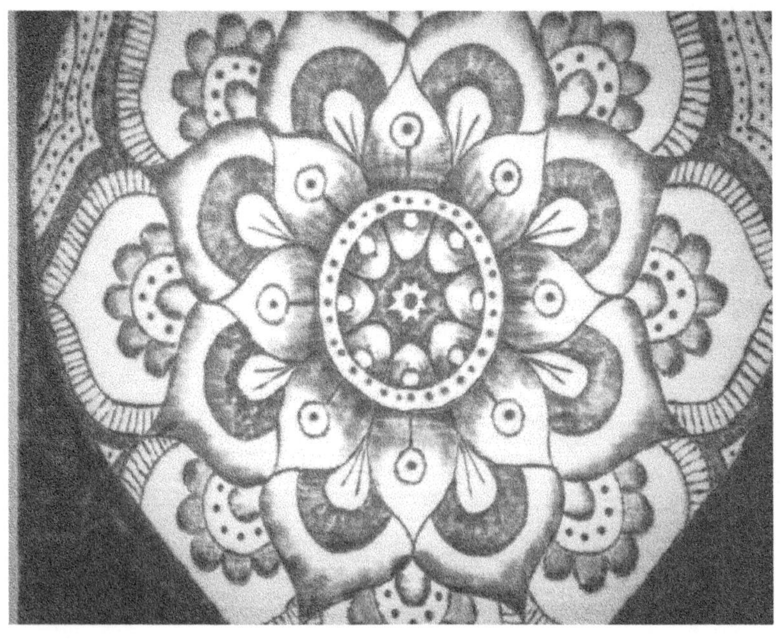

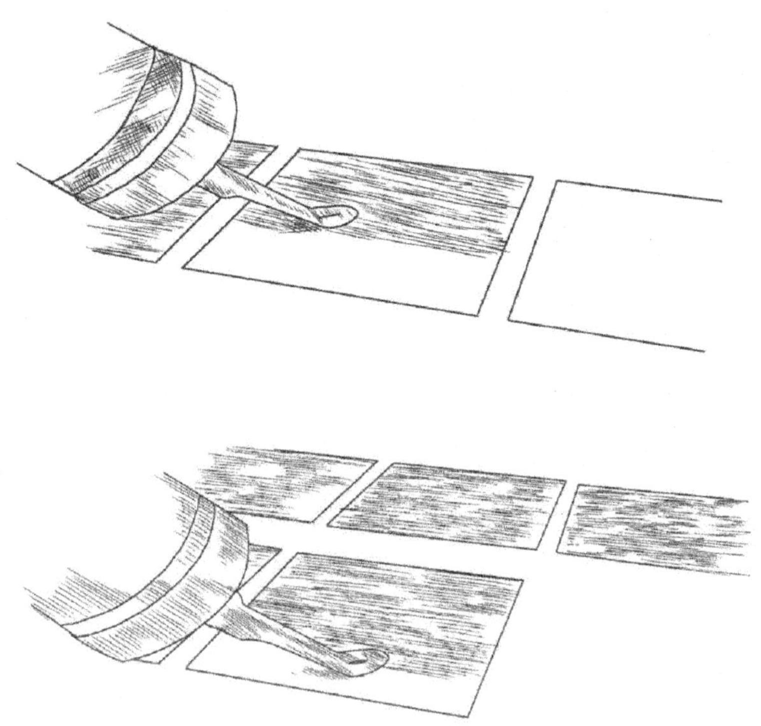

Dot Motion Shading

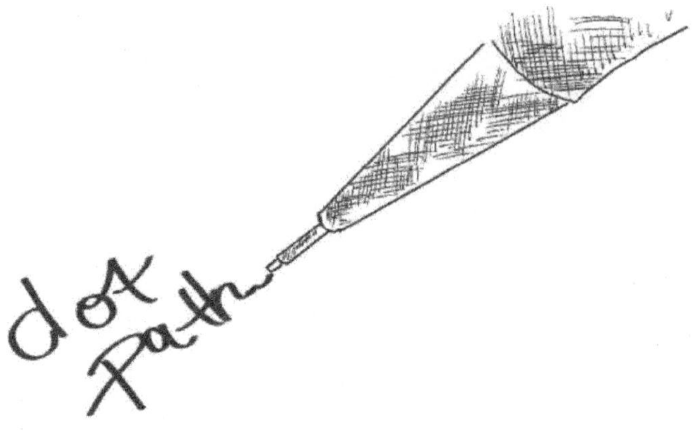

Dot motion shading is a precise method of shading. It takes time and patience. With your heated ball tip at a medium high (3) setting, start dotting the surface of your timber repeatedly, making a lightly shaded dotted design. Leave your ball tip on the surface of the wood for only a small amount of time so that you burn a very lightly shaded area. Make very little contact between your pen and the wood. Next, turn your heat up by .5 (slightly darker pattern) and do the same technique keeping the shade light. As you keep going for the rest of your tonal levels, increase your heat by a half setting. Also, very slowly start increasing the amount of time your tip touches the wood. The longer you tip touches the darker your dots. If your burner doesn't have variable settings, you will have to time how long you burn. The lighter the touch and shorter amount of time for pen to wood, the lighter your dots.

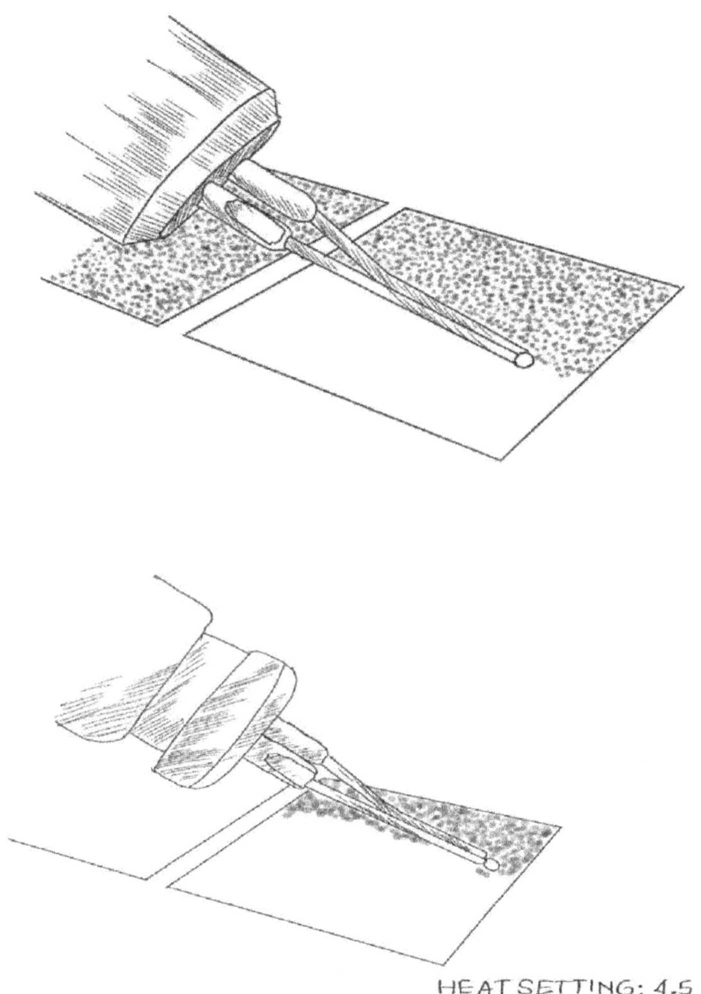

Zig Zag Motion Shading

Zig zag motion shading creates the look of textures specific to the object you are burning, for instance, if you are creating a burn of an animal zig zags are used for short fur. Zig zags are also good for Christmas trees and mountains (see image below). The technique is to literally burn zig zags anywhere from three inches to seven inches (groups are referred to as a zig zag burst). Every new zig zag burst should be offset from the one before. The number of zig zag lines should vary as well as the gap between the lines and the length of the lines.

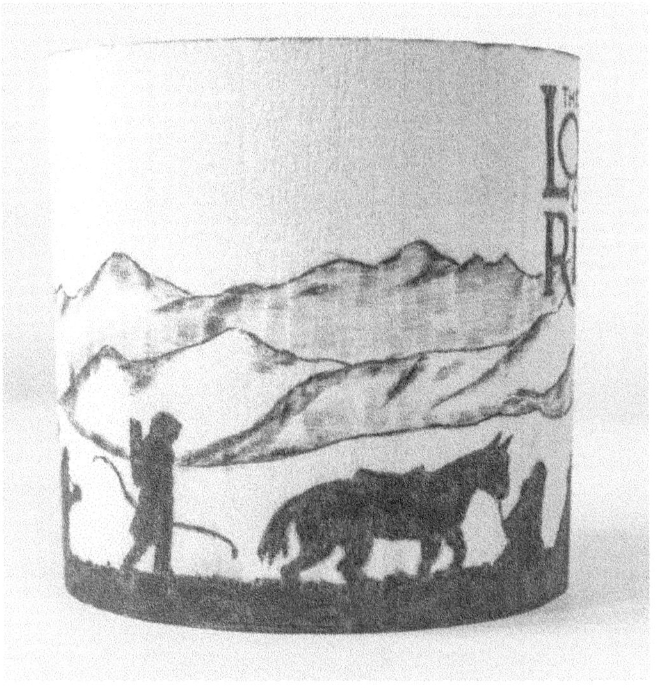

This practice exercise will help you to use these techniques properly on your main projects:

- Sand down a board of timber.

- With a ruler and a pencil draw a box.

- With your wood burning pen use different heat settings and different nibs so you can learn what shade each setting achieves.

- Now start practicing the methods in the boxes

Side Shading

Side shading is a marvelous technique used to bring depth, contour, and color to your art. With the entire side of the pen leaning away from you with very light pressure and then releasing the pressure while moving the pen in any direction, you will produce fantastic shading results. This is an intermediate skill that will come in handy as your craft continues to improve. Using just the tip is the technique for shading smaller areas. Following the same process as used in side shading, changing the angle of the tip will create the level of darkness or lightness you want to achieve.

Line Shading

- *Line shading* is created with a fine point tool. The appearance and the number of lines creates a shading effect visible from a distance. If you burn lines perpendicularly to each other, you will create a dark shaded and more textured background (see image below).

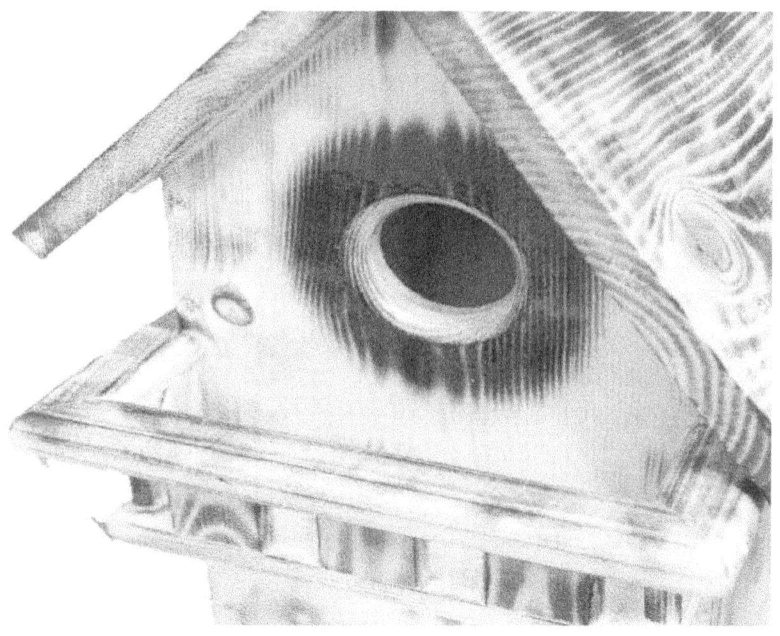

- *Smooth side shading* is created by moving your pen at a constant speed while you are burning your art. The faster you move your pen the lighter the shading, so the slower you move your tip the darker your lines will be.

- *Textured shading technique* is created by very
  quickly or very slowly moving your pen leaving
  no marks from the blade. Any textured pattern
  can be crafted with a loop writing tip by
  making random simple curls or circles which
  are packed together. The tighter a design is
  packed the darker the tone and the denser the
  texture. (Note: When creating texture a
  selected area does not have to be solidly filled,
  there can be open spaces and repeating
  patterns.)

- *Scrubby shading* is made with a *flat spear
  shader* burning random tight circular motions
  or slow and even back-and-forth motions.
  Create several layers of scrubby strokes to
  make the tone deeper in any area. Set the
  burner temperature on medium or medium-
  high, lay the shader's flat against the timber
  and burn small and short touch strokes using a
  pull motion. Slightly lift the shader and burn in
  a random circular pattern to make scrubby
  shades. Repeating the process will give you a
  darker area.

- *Transition side shading technique* is created by
  first moving the pen slowly and then picking up
  speed while you move your pen back and forth.
  This will create shading that graduates from
  dark to light.

- *Combination shading* is when you use more than one technique to burn in the same area. The combination is only limited to your imagination (see image below). Using a circular motion and uniform strokes along with zig zags and contouring creates a beautiful design. Contouring is how you give a design its three-dimensional shape. If you uniformly shade your whole piece it will look flat. Even using a zig zag technique, it is uniform in color. But, if you use a gradient tone, your piece will have a three dimensional appearance. Gradient shading progresses in tone by going from dark to light or vice versa. To achieve a gradient tone you use smooth uniform lines where you gradually increase or decrease your pressure or hand speed to lighten or darken your color.

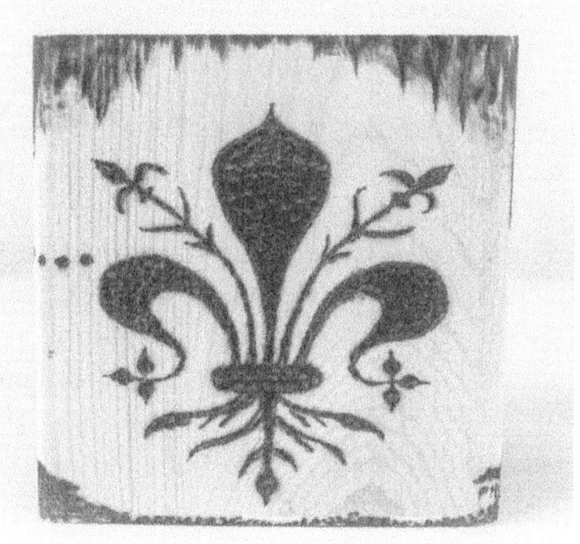

- *Pointillism* technique, simply put, is a group of small dots spaced a certain distance depending on the design the artist wants to achieve. Many tiny dots spaced far apart give a light tone, while medium size dots packed tightly together create a darker town.

- *Dot shading technique* is used to produce a shaded appearance from a distance. Depending on the size of the dot you want to make, use the cone, flow, or miniflow point and with light pressure move in a random direction burning dots as you go along.

- *Basketweave technique* is created by randomly placing lines to make a woven look texture. Group five or six lines parallel and in random directions to each other. On top of the basketweave you can side shade to create extra depth and warmth to your art piece.

- To form a dark ripple effect use the *relief dot technique.* Using the same amount of time for each dot, take the flow or mini flow (depending on the size of the dot you want to create) and in a circle motion place one row of dots. Make sure to complete the circle before you place your second row in a circular motion to the inside of the first row. This technique makes a beautiful contoured effect on your art piece.

- For a beautiful and unique cross stitch appearance use the *counted dot technique.* You can either trace each dot on to your wood in a graph type pattern and then burn them or to mark a graph like pattern onto the wood with a soft pencil. Place the dots 1/16th of an inch apart. This technique makes uniform designs on your piece pleasant to the eye. You are essentially burning a cross stitch instead of sewing one into the wood.

- For a soft, warm, and rich appearance, use the *figure-eight technique.* Using a soft point tip burn eights onto the wood and then burn another eight on top of that in a slightly different direction. Now that you are at the intermediate skill level you should be able to burn your eights together in one fluid motion. For a deeper look, side shade over the eights.

- For a beautiful etched look use the *contour crosshatch technique.* You can pattern over the natural grain of the wood, or an S curve, basically any contour design you want. Crosshatching is accomplished by burning two groups of lines parallel to each other. Afterwhich, burn two groups of slightly arching parallel lines at a 45 degree angle to your first set, and then two sets of lines burned perpendicular to each other. You can again side shade over the crosshatching with varying degrees of pressure to create a deeper or richer depth of shade.

- *Sfumato* (means to tone down or evaporate like smoke) is a technique of blending tones. It is used to soften the transition between patterns or colors. For example, this technique gives way to a smokey look, by creating an illusion with your pen of realistic and dimensional images. Sfumato technique does not use outlines or uses very little outlining to turn designs into patterns of dark to light. This technique is fine shading that produces easy, indiscernible transitions between tones. First, sand your wood until it is very smooth. Using your miniflow point, outline the shapes you want to appear in your design. This outlining will become part of the shading, so keep them very light. Next using your shading point produce the figure eight, crosshatch, or any other background shading technique. Begin by shading the background first by going from light to as dark as you choose. Make sure to not go over the outline you made with your miniflow point. This will show a dark background with white design elements. This is an impressive technique to learn. Next, you can begin to shade the white design elements. Starting with a light shade and gradually moving toward dark, continue to use the shading point and go over the outline made with the mini flow point and into the darkened background areas. This will give the piece that smokey or fading element (Walnut Hollow, 2020). In the meantime, hold your art away from you and make necessary adjustments in the tonal areas. Remember this artwork is to be viewed from a distance.

- ***Solid fill texture*** is used in a wood burning project when an area needs to be completely filled with a solid burn. That specific area may be a graduated shading or one tone. Burning fine lines, or dot patterns create texture that is even and smooth in color.

Texturing

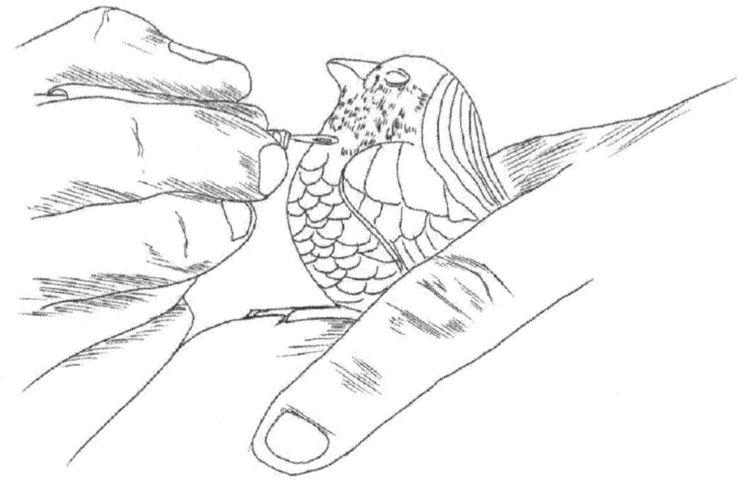

Texturing is an advanced version of shading. It adds a third dimension in your pyrography art. There are three main types of wood burners that can be used to make textures.

Utility Wood Burner

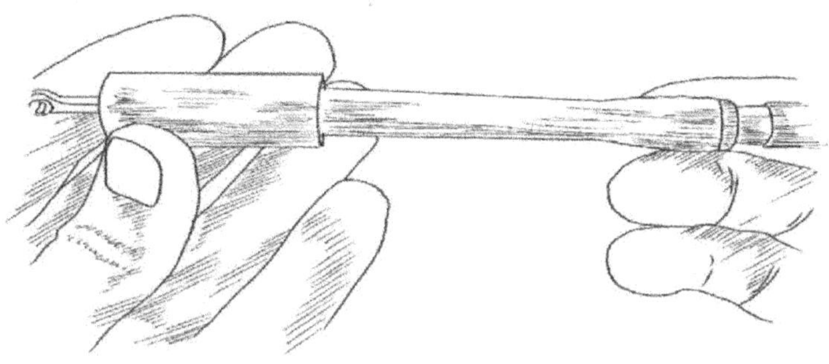

The utility wood burner tool is used to make custom designs which can be used according to your art style. It's mainly used for outer detailing. The utility wood burner creates burned lines, images, and patterns in your project. This burner is used to create outline patterns, shading projects, to fully detailed art. Using a looped or ball tip with middle of the range heat setting, burning just the outlines of any pattern is what this tool does best. With any texture or fill stroke you can combine the tonal value and outlining to shadow and shape your design. This unit works well on burning loosely packed lines and for scrubbie patterns (see image below).

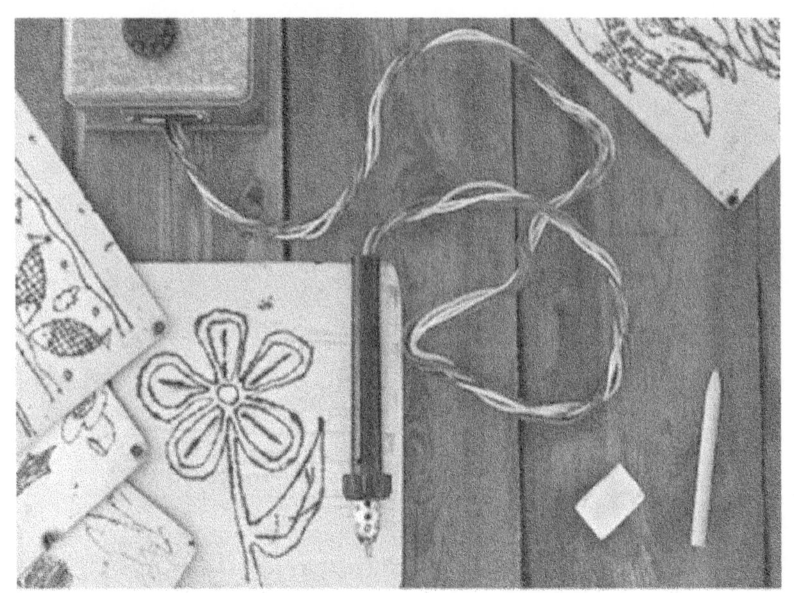

shutterstock.com • 377593228

Walnut Hollow Versa Tool

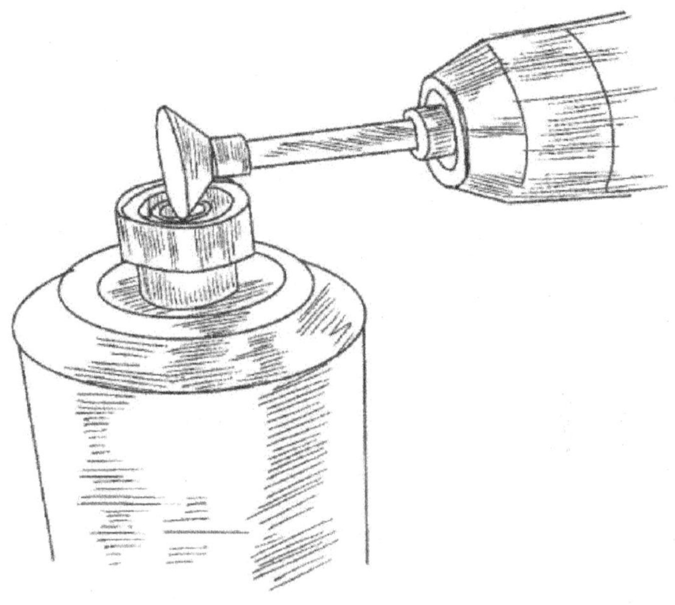

The Walnut Hollow Versa Tool has variable temperature control settings and a comfortable grip. This tool is used to create circular texture on things like eyes. Its universal point achieves most techniques fundamental to wood burning. It has a flow point for dot shading, dots, curves, and writing in cursive. A tapered point is used to make designs that are intricate and it works on multiple surfaces. The tool also comes with a calligraphy point and a shading point for shading sides and larger areas with a light touch of your pen. The mini flow point is used for small dots, circles, intricate designs, and writing in cursive. For cuts and shapes on a variety of species of wood, the hotknife point comes in handy. If you need to join metal use the soldering point (lead free). It also has star, circle, and square stamping points so you can create borders and cool looking patterns on various surfaces. If you are into stencils, place the pattern down on your wood and with a pencil create your outline by using the pulling technique to burn your art. In the image below, the background is worked on birch plywood using a tightly packed scrubbie stroke (small short strokes made with a ball point tip on your burner to make evenly graduated shading) with the spear shader and on a medium-high temperature setting.

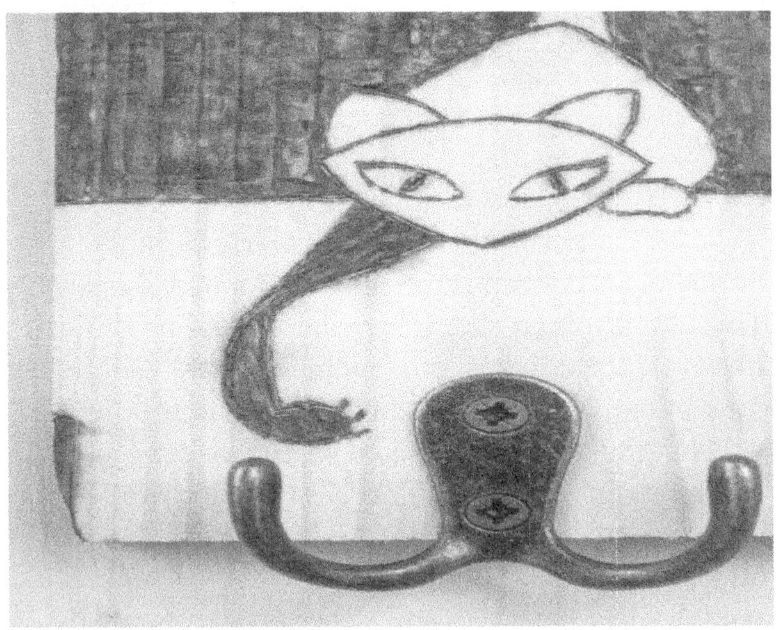

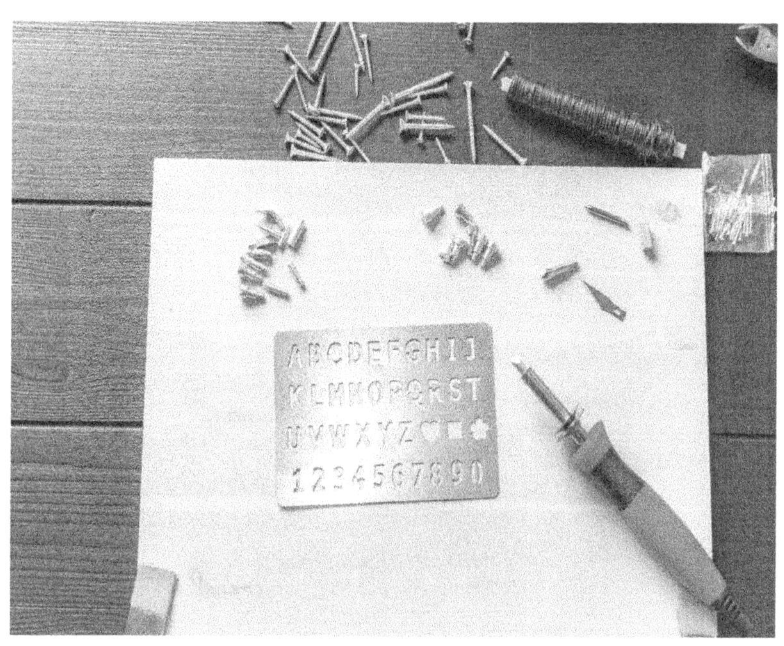

Razertip Pyrographic Burners

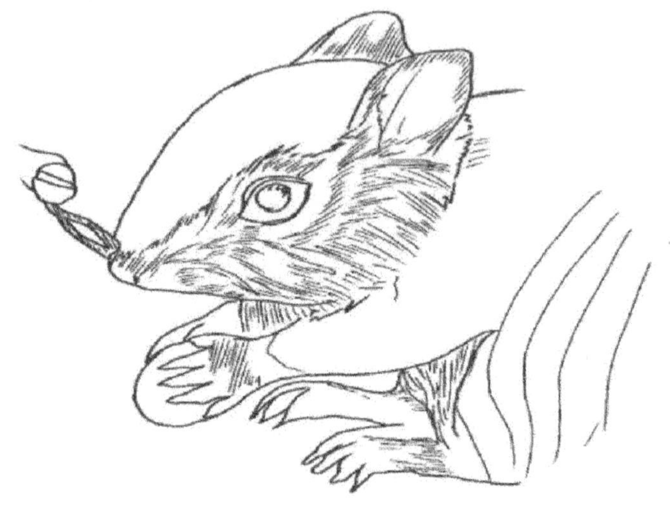

The Razertip Pyrographic burner gives fantastic heat stability even if you are repeating the same lines. Each attached pen has its own temperature control which means you can switch pens without having to wait for one to cool down. The Razertip burner comes with *fixed tip* pens or *interchangeable tip* pens. This tool is used to create circular textures. The 'sharp' tip can burn up to 120 lines per inch and is perfect for crafting feathers, hair, and other fine details. The 'wide line' sharp tips do not burn quite as finely but are great for texturing. The Razertip burner's shading tips have rounded sides so they do not carve into your wood surface. They come with spear and spoon tip shaders. Razertip burners have various stylus and writing tips such as ball tips and wire tips in all sizes.

Another fascinating feature of the Razertip burner is its *feather former* which lets you burn a barbed texture and define a feather in seconds. To complement the feather former is the *quill making tip* for layering feathers so they look raised with a reduced need for sanding (see image below). The split-making tips are made to burn the subtle fissures in feathers or hair or fur. The split-making tip is a great practice for the intermediate level wood burner. The Razertip kit also has special-purpose tips for burning serrated design patterns or scary tooth-like designs. If you are into burning alligators, lizards, or dinosaurs, or dragons, use the customized scale tip. Using fixed tipped pens lets you work with your fingers closer to the wood, allowing very good control for fine details.

Razertip tool can be used for stamping or signing your projects. It can almost always be set at a low heat and comes with an extra handpiece. That way if you have to use high heat and the grip gets too hot just switch it for the other one. Let the hot one cool for around ten minutes. Never use any sandpaper, rouge, emery, or other abrasives to clean your tip, it will prematurely wear it out and cause carbon buildup faster. The hand piece allows you to reach further by sliding the grip on the pen back. If you want consistent heating, make sure to burn in areas free from wind or air conditioning draft. Even a light draft will cause your tip to cool.

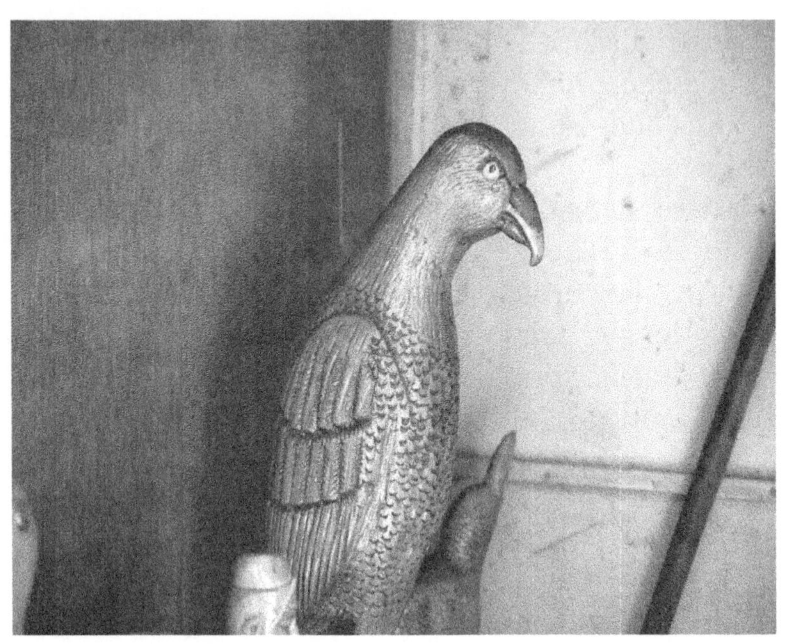

Chapter 3:
Wood Burning, Colors and Much More

Coloring and wood burning are a fantastic match. At the intermediate level coloring your projects will add life to the natural tones of your wood. While you do not have to color in wood burning, combining the two techniques can create stunning results. Watch out for any suggestions for using water-based paints as the moisture will make the grain in the wood raise.

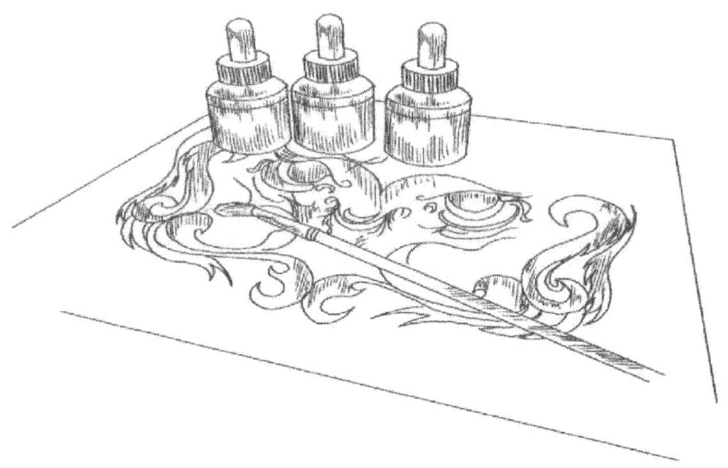

This project is a great example of how to turn your wood burning art piece into an even more artful masterpiece. To make this project come to life, you need to be creative and passionate.

Materials

- A wooden board according to your requirements

- Sanding paper of 400-grit

- A wood burning tool according to your requirements

- A printout of your art and tracing paper

- Pen or pencil for tracing your art

- Paint brushes (preferably synthetic of 00, 3, 8 or 12 size)

- Some acrylic colors of your choice

Steps

- Use sandpaper to take the grains out of your wooden board and make it smooth.

- Then use your pen/pencil and your printout of the art piece you would like to create, and the tracing paper, and your board to trace your art.

- Then draw an outline of your traced art with the help of a wood burning tool.

- Use any techniques used in the book to fill in the gaps of your art.

- Apply a thin layer of water on your outline with the help of a wide brush.

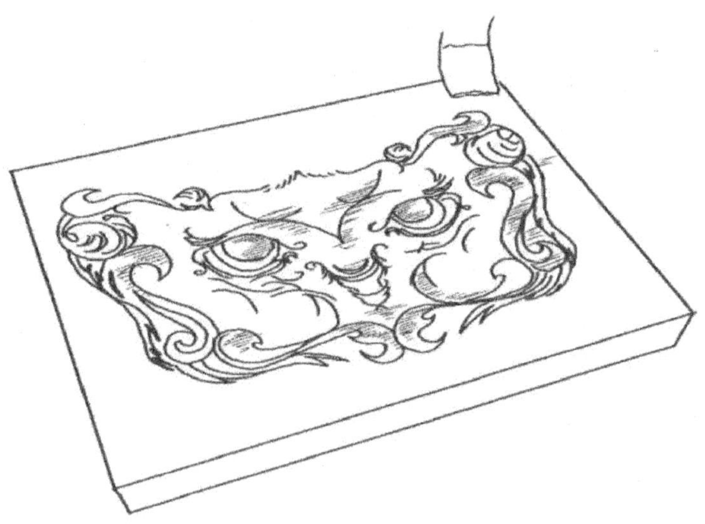

- Then use your 00 brush to fill the colors according to your requirements. As the surface of wood is wet the color will spread evenly.

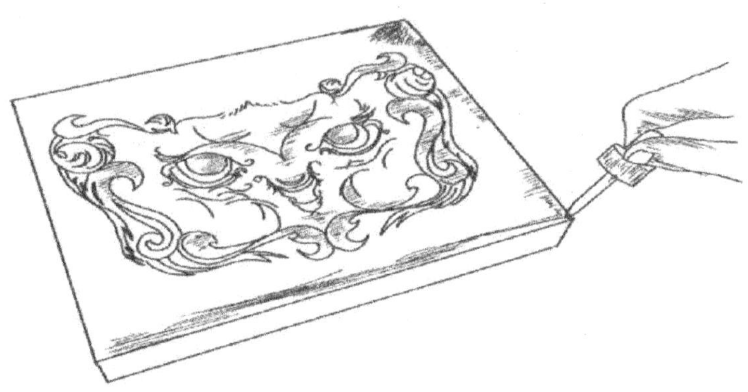

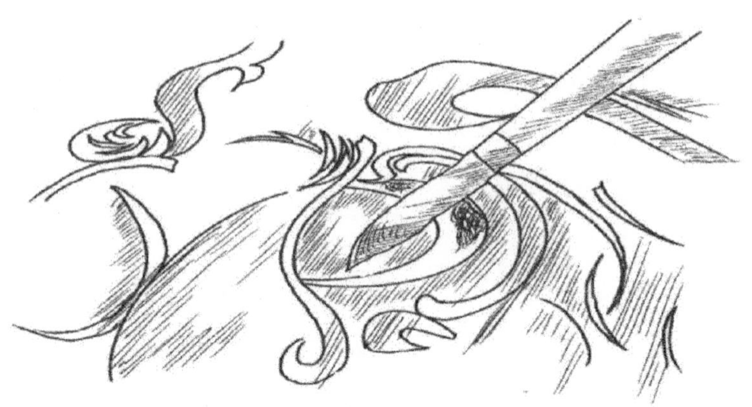

Choosing Your Pattern

It is obviously important for you to have a design that pleases you. Some of the essential principles for you know include harmony, balance, repetition, contrast, unity, and proportion. These principles will guide you toward creating a piece of art that has classic beauty. When deciding your design start sketching on paper until you create what you are striving for. It make take several sketches before you perfect your design. After your design is perfected transfer it onto tracing paper. You may even want to practice color combinations on some scrap wood or paper before committing them to the good surface. You can make your patterns on your computer using a variety of computer programs. This can make it easy. You can download any picture from the internet and if you're monogramming you can use whatever size and type font you like. Using programs like Powerpoint you can multiply copies and change the size, or do other image manipulations of the object you copied. For example, if you want to burn your logo into a wooden coaster, you can scan it and make it into all different designs until you find the one you want. Then, simply print it. If you use tracing paper, you can simply put it over your coaster and hold it up to a light bulb to gauge the size. At this stage of your learning process color can be added to create differing dimensions and lighting. Pressure techniques can enhance creations making 3D effects in your piece of art. Untreated hardwoods that are light in color such as birch, basswood, or sycamore are fine grain and used most often. After the pattern is burned into the wood, designs are often colored. The equipment used should allow you to employ an assortment of brushstrokes needed to burn the different effects you envision in your creation. Once your wood piece is cut to the size you desire, check it out to make sure it does not have any dents or unwanted markings. (Tip: If there are shallow dents or nicks, moisten a cloth, fold it in half, and place it onto the dent. Next, take a hot iron and press it down on the cloth. Keep doing that until the dents raise and then let the wood dry). Next you want to sand the wood with sandpaper until it has a smooth finish. (Tip: Wrap your sandpaper around a wooden block with a flat side to get an even surface on your wood piece).

After a design is chosen, figure out the size you want to use for your project. You can size your project based on wood that you may have already. Cut out your design and tape it to the carbon paper and then tape it to your piece of timber. With your pen and a steady hand, trace your design's outline. After that follow your outline, burning as you go. Stick in the direction of grain as best as you can. Carefully, fill in any spots with your shading tip and finish with a nice sheen or shellac. Wood burning patterns in just about every category you can imagine are abundantly displayed on the internet. Also, there are many wood burning books with patterns, border designs, and stencils on sale anywhere books can be found. You can browse through any of these places to find inspiration for your projects or even combine several of them to create your own inspired ideas. (Note: Using patterns or stencils does not mean it is not your own. Everytime a stencil or pattern is used in wood burning, it has the crafter's own unique signature). When you decide which pattern or stencil you like, remember not to 'bite off more than you can chew'. Stick to the intermediate skill level so your patterning or designing matches your technical abilities. Take into serious consideration the amount of detail in the design. Very tiny details such as really fine lines or major textural differences or extreme shading will all still be there when you advance your skill set. Getting there is the fun part. Also, very important is to consider whether or not you have all of the tools, nibs, and tips necessary for each individual project.

Photorealism Using Sfumato Technique

Photorealism technique creates likeness images of people, places, and things you have taken a picture of to aid you in your creative expression. Try to use large images of at least 8 x 10 inches. Run the photo through a copy machine with it on its lightest level. You can put the machine on different settings and make multiple copies to give you a better idea of how light or dark you want your tones to be. Consider using basswood because it is light, soft, and easy to work with. Whichever wood you use, make sure it is one without noticeable grains.

Sand the wood until it is completely smooth. Center the copy of your black and white picture and transfer the image in the usual manner. Only trace the main outline and then lightly erase the graphite lines. Next, use your miniflow point to outline the main shapes in your design. Constantly look back and forth at your photo copies to guide you in the process. Use any of your side shading techniques to enhance the depth and contour of your background. Once you finish the burning, look at your piece from a distance in case you want to add more personal touches. If you see any stubborn lines you could not erase, use fine sandpaper to get them out.

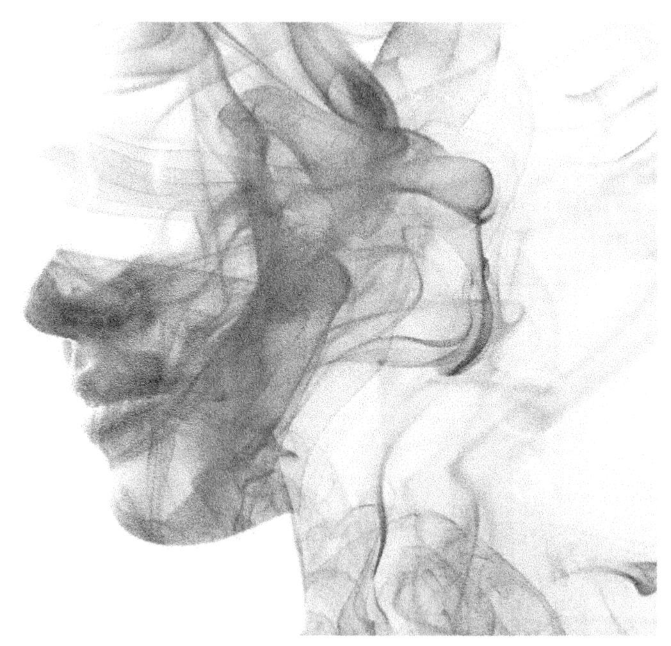

Stencils

Burning beautiful designs and patterns into wood using stencils will help you create just about any design your imagination can conjure up. The following steps will teach you how to use stencils when crafting your wood.

- Sand your wood in the direction of the grain and then wipe it off well ensuring there is no wood dust left on the surfaces.

- With the ink side down, place a piece of graphite paper where you want your design. Use low-tack tape (removeable) and tape the image into place so it doesn't slide while you are burning.

- Place your choice of metal stencil on top of the graphite paper.

- Trace the outside of the stencil on to the graphite paper, and then remove the paper.

- With your desired image now transferred, follow the stencil outlines with your wood burning tool.

- Using a pencil eraser, remove any lines made by the graphite that are still visible.

- Using your oil pencils, starting with light colors, color the pattern.

- Varnish your piece by gently applying the wood finish as to not run the colors together. You can repeat this process over again several times (avoid one large coat).

Chapter 4:
Pyrography Easter Eggs

Easter is such an enjoyable holiday for crafting. Easter eggs are the perfect project for wood burning and for having an amazing, creative good time! When finished, this project will be an adorable table setting or great fun for an Easter egg hunt. The best part is that you can use them again next year and the year after that. Every year! Getting them out and hiding and finding them can become a treasured family tradition.

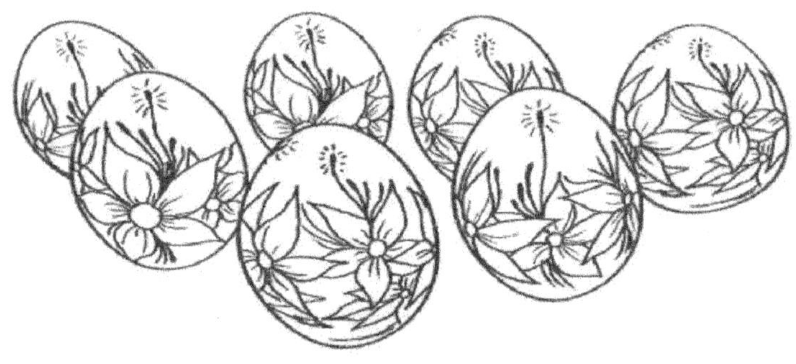

Read below to design your own wooden Easter eggs! You can follow the steps below, and you can also use a regular egg dying kit, but use vinegar not water and leave the wooden egg in the dye for a few minutes and then let them dry. Then follow the steps below. If you want to burn names or any other words, use a pencil and trace the word onto the egg using graphite paper or a light pencil mark. Trace it really dark and then push it graphite side down and scratch the back so it leaves a guide for you to burn.

Materials

- Egg shaped wood

- 400-grit sanding paper

- Wood burning tool

- Spear tip and flat tip for the wood burner

- Pencil (3b)

- Wood painting colors

- Paint brush (00 and 7 size)

Steps

- Use the 400-grit sanding paper to smooth the surface of the wooden egg.

- Use the pencil to draw a basic flower on the wooden egg with the use of a hand and circular stencil (see image below).

- Then use the woodburner with the spear tip to make an outline of your design.

- Then use your flat tip to give a shade to your outline on the outside for a soothing texture.

- Then take your size 7 brush and apply a small layer of water on the wood.

- Then use your 00 paint brush to make a colored outline of your design.

- Then use your size 7 paint brush to fill in the colors. Don't overuse the colors as the colors will spread evenly because of the thin layer of water.

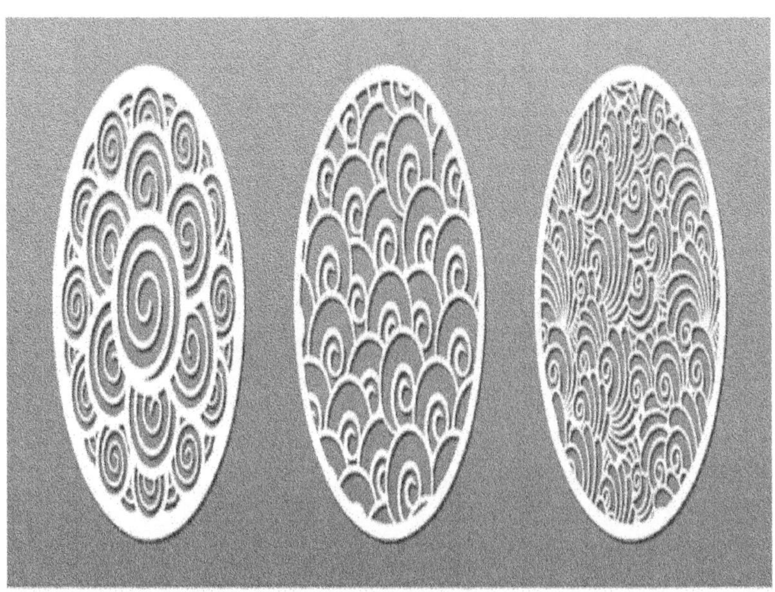

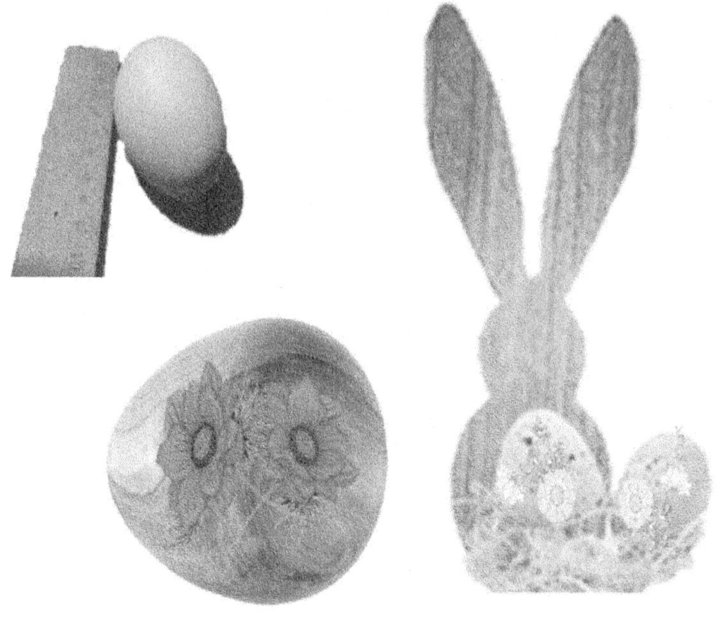

If you already have your eggs waiting for your artwork, think about what designs or patterns would best suit that piece. Avoid trying to "make" something work. You want your finished project to look comfortable. For example, if you are burning a geometric pattern around all sides of the egg, the pattern eventually has to meet or end at a certain point. The wrap-around pattern needs to be seamless.

Graphite Paper

If you decide to use graphite paper for this project follow these steps:

- Center the pattern and attach it to the piece with tape.

- Slide a piece of the graphite paper between the wood and the pattern.

- Use a pencil to shade in on the graphite paper the image you desire to transfer to the wood.

- The graphite transferred to the wood is where you will burn.

- Set up your burning in its wire stand with the heat turned up. You want to be able to scorch the wood.

- Moving in a slow and consistent technique, move your hand in the direction away from the tip of the burner. Here's some extra tips:

  - Using a long point works like a pen point.

  - The flow tip keeps the heat on high with a constant flow allowing consistency.

  - For more control you can use a tapered tip.

Tip: Practicing your craft on cheap or extra pieces of wood can help you realize how your style of going to affect the wood. Try new and different techniques when you practice to hone in your skills. Even if the wood seems smooth, start with a quick sanding using fine-grit paper. This will help you to have the best surface to work on. The smoother the better!

Adding Color

To add color to your egg design use watercolor pencils because when you dip them in alcohol the color dissolves into a paint. Regular colored pencils only provided a tinted color. Before you moisten your pencil tip color your design with the pencil dry. You can use any colors you want from transparent to intensely bright colors. After you color your design, put a little bit of regular rubbing alcohol in a dish. Then soak your paint brush in it. You can use a white watercolor pencil to color your shades to a bit more of a pastel. If you are looking for a solid white use acrylic paint, but mix it with a small amount of rubbing alcohol. You can even use a gold paint pen, which adds a real holiday look. After you have finished coloring your eggs and letting them dry, it is time to varnish. Varnishing will bring the colors out vibrantly and at the same time protect them from scratches. After completing the color stage and letting it dry, it is wise to varnish your project. It is suggested to use lacquer because it doesn't turn yellow, it dries quickly, and if you want it can be removed fairly easily using lacquer thinner. You can also use shellac, linseed oil, or polyurethane. You may also want to add color to your piece for added dimension. First use a spray sealant on the wood. Oil-colored pencils are perfect for this type of coloring (Walnut Hollow, 2020). They will complement your art by not filling the wood burned lines like using paint would. After you color your project, use the spray sealant again so that the finished product will not smear or bleed. You can pencil with light strokes for a pastel effect or heavy strokes for a solid color effect. For shadows use dark colored pencils and for highlights use light colored pencils. Another neat trick is to use mineral spirits atop of a cotton swab for blending your colors together. Once you are happy with the finished product, use a non-yellowing water-based varnish. Then lightly sand using fine grade sandpaper once the varnish is dry, and then wipe it with your handy tack rag. Tack rags are special rags specifically made to remove loose particles of dirt, lint, and dust. This will protect your work from dust and moisture.

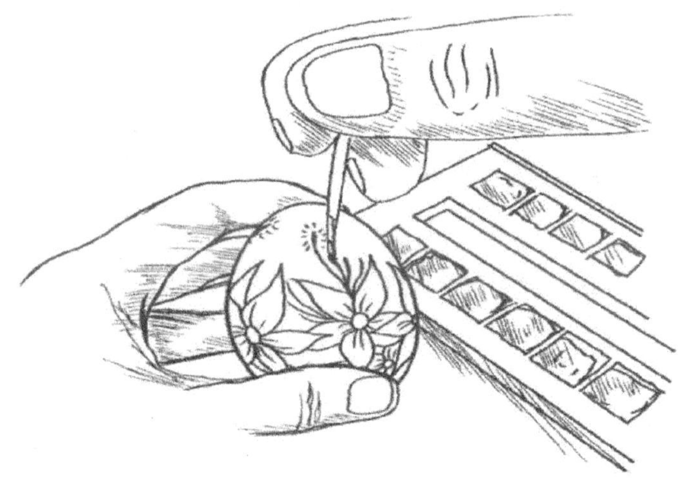

Very often a wood burned piece of art needs not a single thing added for it to be beautiful, but for some projects you may want to add a bit of color to your burned design. A pop of color can add a striking effect, or liven it up a bit, if that is your choice. There are many ways to add color to your wood project. When using *watercolor paints*, look for a good quality of watercolor paints. The varying wood surfaces and its density may affect the watercolor. *Watercolor pencils* are fairly easy to control and allow for more detailed work. First, color in your design with the pencil and then use a water brush to blend. Depending on your design, with *acrylic paints* you can layer your paint thickly or thinly. The aspect of adding differing shades of color makes acrylic paint a decided option. Because it is slightly thick it is easier to control and can be applied to any wood species. *Markers* are another option of the addition of color to your project. Like watercolor paint, markers can also run on soft wood so make sure to test it first. Markers make precision designing possible. Other ways to color your project include: different shades of wood, chalk, food dyes, crayons, oil paints, and pastels.

Here are some techniques for adding color to your wood burning project:

- Pick a wood surface that suits your needs.

- Burn your design onto the surface of your project.

- Pick your colors keeping in mind that some mediums are very wet, such as watercolor, and may run outside of your lines. This is especially true if you use a soft wood such as pine.

Chapter 5:
Welcome Sign

The outside of your home is the first experience people have when they come to visit. A welcome sign is a great first impression. Visitors will know immediately that you are an enthusiastic crafting home right away when you have a beautiful welcome sign that you made using your wood burning skills . This project is also designed to advance your familiarity with your wood burning tools and how different species of timber feel when burned.

For this project pine is used. Pine is chosen because it has both soft and hard grain. As you are working, you will see how simple it is to burn the soft grains too deeply and the challenges of getting the same level of darkness in the hard grains. This project is meant to advance your skill level. You will be adjusting the settings on your tool as you go along, or if you do not have heat settings, you will learn how to change your speed quickly to get the right effect. Practice with your burner on pieces of scrap wood and you won't go wrong. The main goal for this project, other than a gorgeous sign, is to get to know how pine feels when you are burning it.

About the timber: For this welcome sign the letters will be in a dark deep burn with no shading. This is why pine is the best choice. The lack of consistency in the grain pattern will not be a problem with lettering, and bigger pine canvases are not difficult to find, and they are affordable.

Materials

- Wood burning tool with a straight edge tip and a round tip 2

- Safety equipment: mask, fan and finger guards

- Template

- 18″ (46-cm) round pine canvas

- Erasable carbon paper

- Pencil

- Tape

- Weathered gray stain

- Gloves

- Black gloves in wooden background

- 2 sponge brushes

- Wood accent flourishes (get at any hobby shop)

- White or cream acrylic craft paint

- Medium paintbrush

- Spar Urethane by Minwax

- Wood glue

- Sawtooth hanger with screws

- Phillips head screwdriver

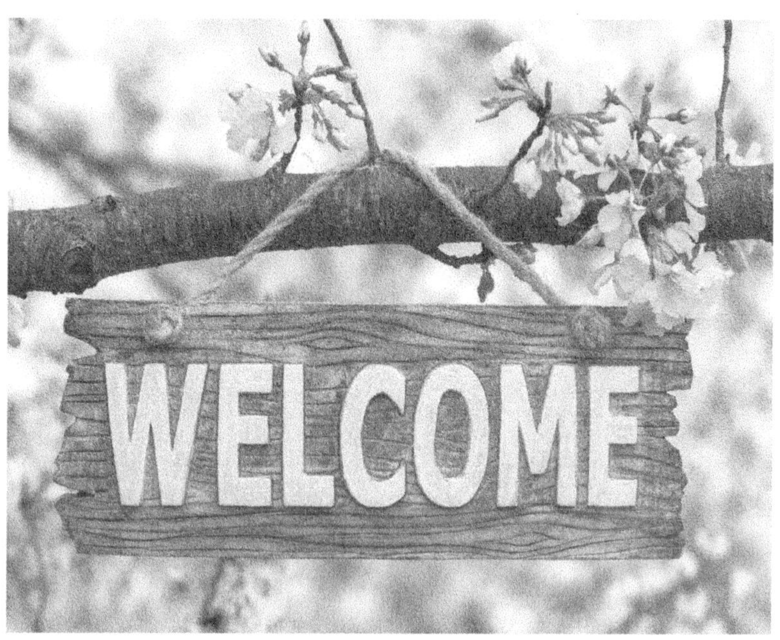

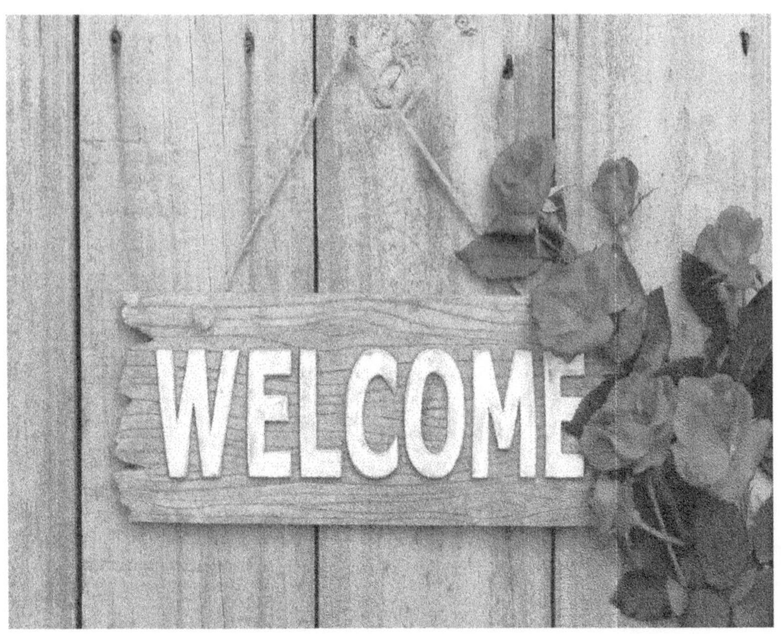

Steps

- Use a straight edge tip on your burning tool. Place the heat to a medium-high. Let your tool preheat while you ready your workplace and wood piece. Your lines will be large, so if you are comfortable you can burn at a quicker pace. (Note: If you do not have heat settings on your tool, you can still craft this sign. The default heat setting will be okay for burning large lines faster. If your tip gets too heated, just hold it in front of a fan for a minute). As discussed in Chapter Two, safety first. Have the essentials: mask, finger guards, and fan.

- When your burner is ready, burn the outlines of all of the letters. By doing so, it is easier to fill them in later and it also makes the letters have a clean edge. Follow the carbon lines on your piece until every letter's outline is burned.

  - You can draw letters freehand or use a template on wood. Just use a pencil and stencil! You can use your wood burner freehand but it is not as easy as having a pattern to follow.

  - Transfer your letters to the wood. Remember, you can print a design off of your computer and transfer it to the wood surface. Just place carbon paper on your wood piece and put your design on top. Use your point and trace the design making sure it is carbon side down.

  - Decide which tip to use. For small details use a small tip and for thick or large letters use a bigger tip. Some kits come with specialty tips. These specific tips have designs on their tip surface that can transfer to your project in a stamp like manner. Tips come in letters, too. Note that when using special stamp letters, you have to switch your tip for each letter. Please, don't forget how hot the tip is. There are also various shaped tips for crafting different types of shading or lines. There are wedge shaped tips that come to a point on one side for burning straight lines. There is a way to transfer photocopies onto wood using your wood burner tip. The images are manufactured just for this technique. Put the image face down and gradually heat the back of the paper with your 'image transfer tip'. The hot tip transfers the image to the wood. This process does not work with copies from an inkjet printer. It only works with photocopies. ** You also have to have the special tip for your pen. If your kit did not come with the specialized tip, try contacting the kit's manufacturer to see if they have one available.

- Heat up your equipment and make sure it is warm enough before you start burning so your work will be well defined. For solid outlining, your burner should be set at around 700 degrees Fahrenheit (370° C). For lighter shading lower the temperature to midrange.

- Practice with the degree of pressure on the wood piece you chose to see the different effects; usually, with a firm grip but pressing lightly does the job. The more pressure the deeper and darker the letters. Move at a steady pace across the wood's surface, using a continuous speed. If you vary your speed it will change the contour of your lines. The slower you burn the deeper and darker it will be. Becoming skilled with consistent lines takes practice.

- Trace each letter by beginning with the letter's outline. Using a smooth motion try not to stop until you complete the entire letter if you want consistent and smooth lines. End your strokes at the end of each letter. For instance, the R letter can take three strokes: the loop at the top, the straight upright line, and the protruding line on the lower right end *R*. The O letter is done in a single stroke **O** (Lowes Editorial Team, 2020).

- If you have designed thick letters you may have to go over filling them more than once after you have them outlined. If this is the case use a larger burner tip, especially for filling in large areas that take a long time.

- Once you have created your letters, you can embellish your piece further by adding swirl designs, vines, flowers, etc. Your kit may have come with a heart patterned design stamp or other fun designs.

- Now that you have outlined all of your letters, turn your burner off to let it cool down. Switch to the number 2 round tip. Let your burner heat back up to medium heat. (Note: pine wood burns fast and has a lot of give, so you have to burn quickly so the wood does not scorch or become too dark where you do not want it).

- Fill in the letter outlines with a straight-line pattern. Straight- line patterns add a neat texture rather than just using a flat burn (see image below) .

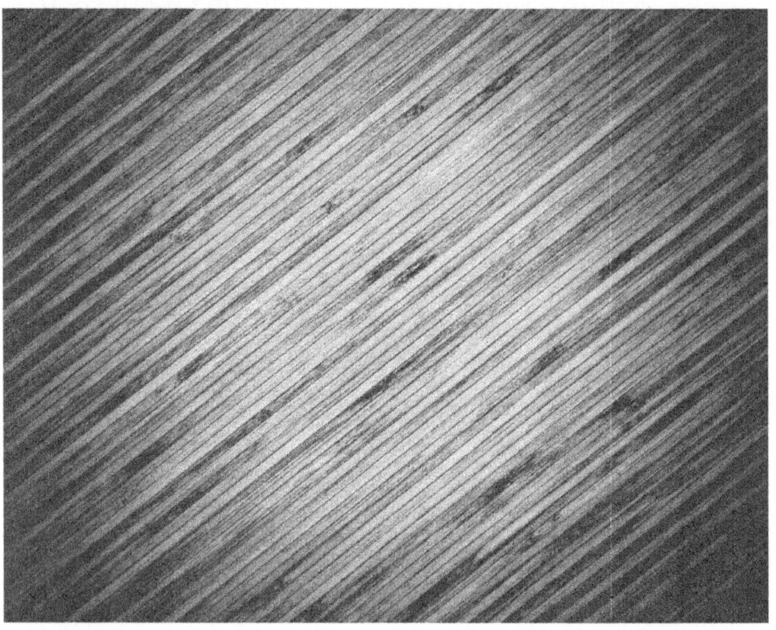

- Start with burning straight horizontal lines inside the letter W. Then do the same with each letter.

  - For the **W**, put your tip inside the left edge of the W and pull it over the wood's surface to the right side of the W's edge. Now you have a straight horizontal line.

- Using the tip of the burner, just under the first horizontal line, drag it over to the right side again. The result we are looking for is the burned lines to connect so the whole surface is created. Do this over and over until you have filled the whole letter with straight horizontal lines.

- Do the same burning technique inside of each letter until you have filled them in completely. (**Tip**: If by accident you burn outside of the lines, it is fixable. When you are finished, go back to using your straight edge tip, and trace along the outer lines already there. When finished the inside pattern, go back to using your straight edge tip and add another line to cover up the spots where you accidentally burned outside of the lines).

- First, stain the sign in a grayish or weathered gray stain. The pine's soft grain will really absorb the stain and the hard grains will repel it just a little. This adds contrast and gives your piece a homey farmhouse look.

- Wearing gloves and using a sponge brush loaded with stain, apply the stain following the wood grain.

- **Tip**: **If you want to mix your own gray color, stain your wood with a dark walnut.

Mix 1 part white paint with 1 part water.
Then paint long strokes of the white wash
with a paint brush, then rub over that with a
staining cloth, making sure it is free of lint,
smear the whitewash mixture into your
timber and allow it to fully dry. After it is
dry you can very lightly sand in sporadic
places to add character.

- As your stained wood is drying, embellish the small accent parts with paint.

  - Paint the front of each accent piece, let them dry, and paint the backs. After drying, varnish.

- Varnish the front and back of your welcome sign. Fill your sponge brush with varnish and coat your sign and any accent pieces.

- Position your accent pieces around the sign and glue them in place. Allow to dry.

- Use a 25 pound sawtooth hanger and center it on the back of your sign and screw it into place.

Chapter 6:
Fire Epoxy Table

What's better than adding value to your life through your art. Tables are an essential part of our life, we always seem to use them on a day to day basis. If you showcase a piece of art on a table which you have made from scratch, every time you pass by it you will admire it and be proud of yourself.

Safety Disclaimer: Please pay extra precaution while handling fire, and wear some safety equipment like glasses, gloves, face shield and clothes that fully cover your body.

Material

- Thick 2.5-inch wooden slab

- A blow torch

- Epoxy resin 1 liter

- Epoxy clear polish

- Table legs

- 1600-grit sanding paper

- Measurements of your wooden slab to make a small box for your epoxy to settle.

- Lay down a wooden slab on an insulated surface.

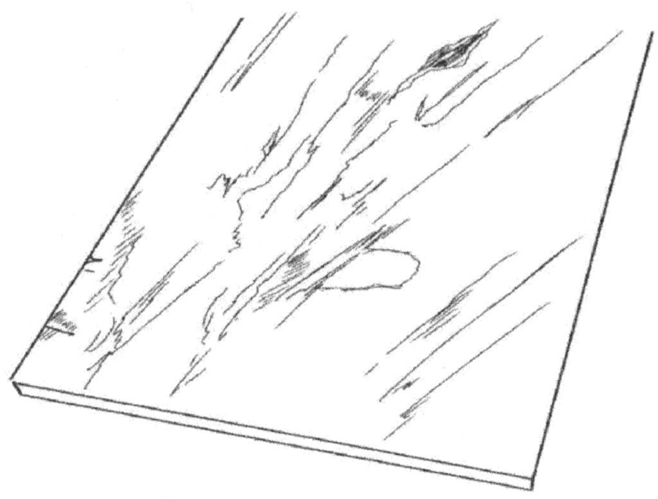

- Take out your blow torch and set it to high flames

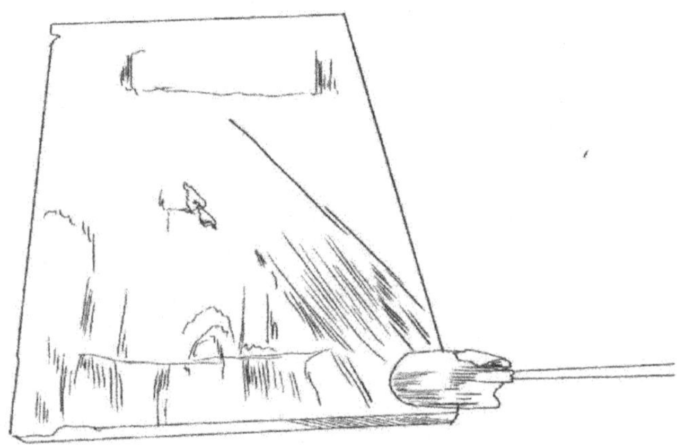

- Start burning your wooden slab evenly, including the sides of the slab. There really is not an incorrect way to burn a slab, as long as you are safe about it. You will need to burn some areas more than others. You can burn aggressively to get a deep char texture. Note: While burning the slab it may cup up in your direction, but when you burn the opposite side it will bring that cup down. So, in theory if you burn the same amount on both sides the end result will be a flat slab. Get out your leveler and check it out. You can reverse cupping by burning more in certain areas. Douse your slab with water when you're finished so it does not continue smoldering. Just make sure it is completely dry before you move on to the epoxy phase.

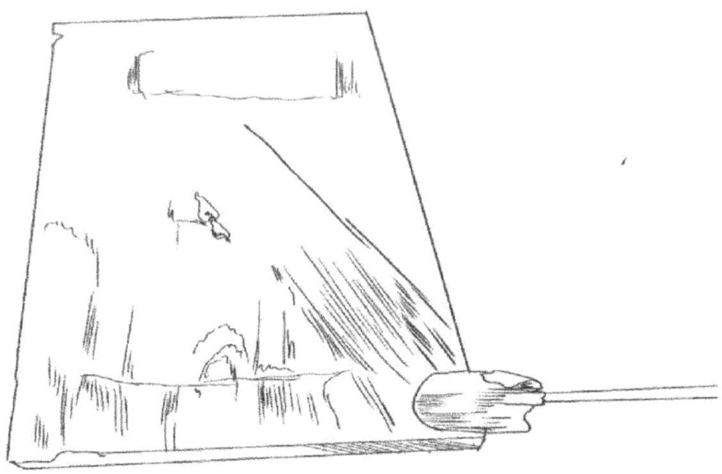

- Seal the wood that you have charred using epoxy (Liquid Glass epoxy is suggested). Saturate the wood you have charred with a brush (don't let it pool yet on the top). (Note: The reason for this is that pooled epoxy on top of plain burned wood has loads of bubbles, so the wood should be stabilized first with epoxy, then it can be submerged completely in the epoxy with hardly any bubbles).

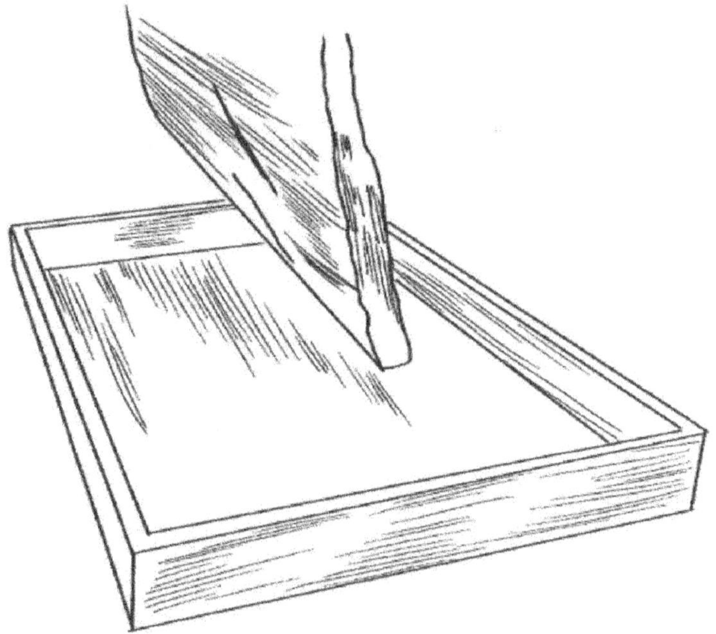

- On one side, brush the epoxy until the wood is totally saturated.

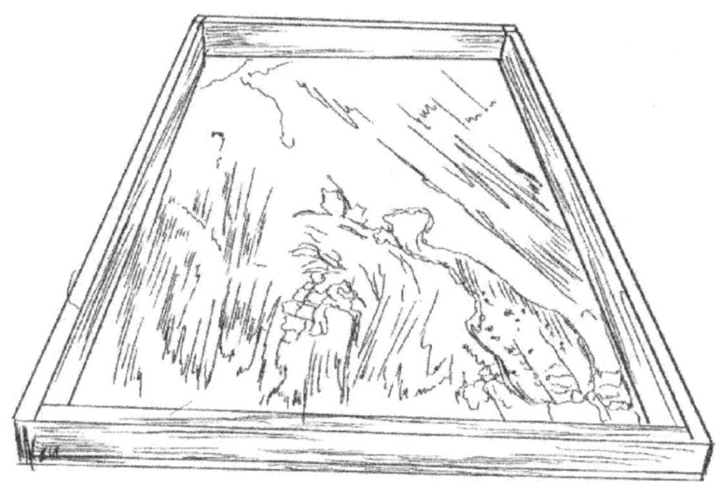

- Flip over the slab and put it in the mold.

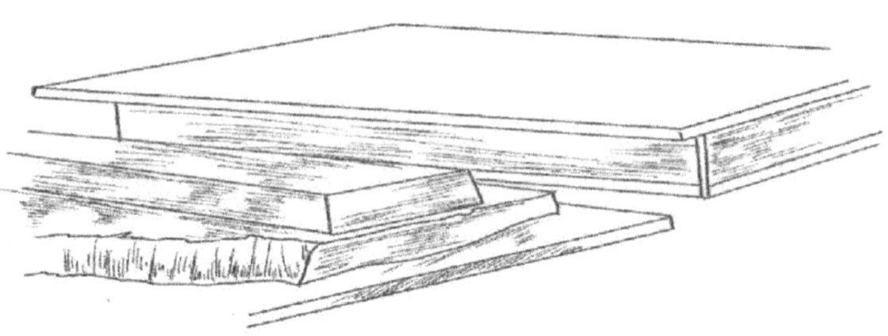

- On the other top side do the saturation process again while it is in the mold.

- Leave it for at least three days.

- Now prepare an appropriate box for your wooden slab to put in as shown in the diagram.

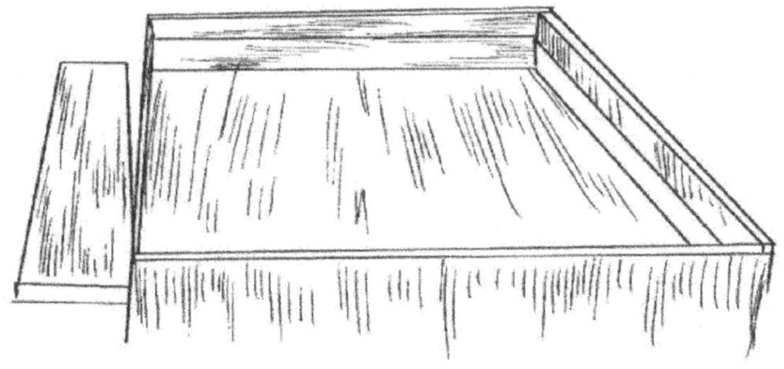

- Now that your wood is epoxy sealed you can go for your deep pour. This is what gives the piece a 3D appearance and good depth (see image below).

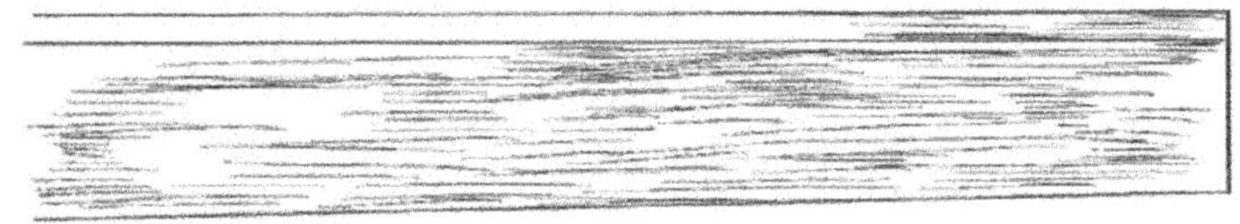

- Whichever epoxy you decide to use, make sure to follow the mixing instructions. Then pour it over your piece submerging the whole piece by approximately ¼ inch.

- After pouring, cover your box to keep any debris or dust out while it sits and cures for the next four days.

- After four days take out your slab from the box where the epoxy is settled.

- Getting your table flat after curing depends on how level your box was. You can probably just sand it flat by hand or you can use an orbital sander. To get your table flat, run your table through a planer.

- Using 320-grit sand your charred epoxy table.

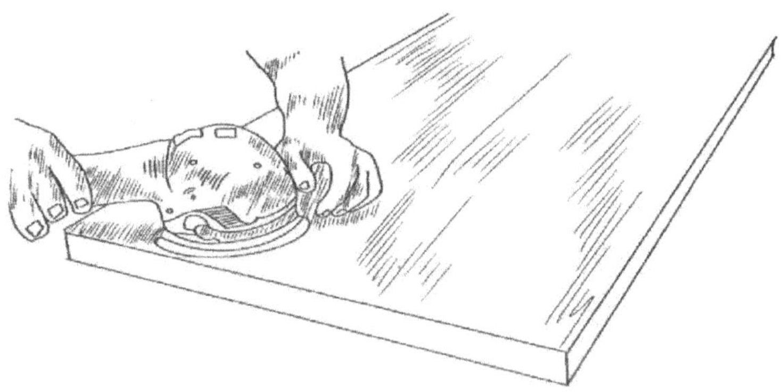

- For the top coat, you can use epoxy or table top resin. This is different from what you used for the deep pour.

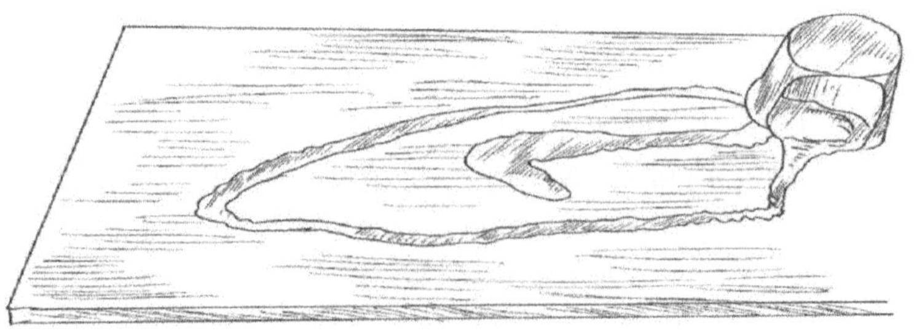

- Warm the epoxy up in a water bath prior to mixing. Simply put the containers in a sink of hot water. This will make it thinner and it will easily self-level.

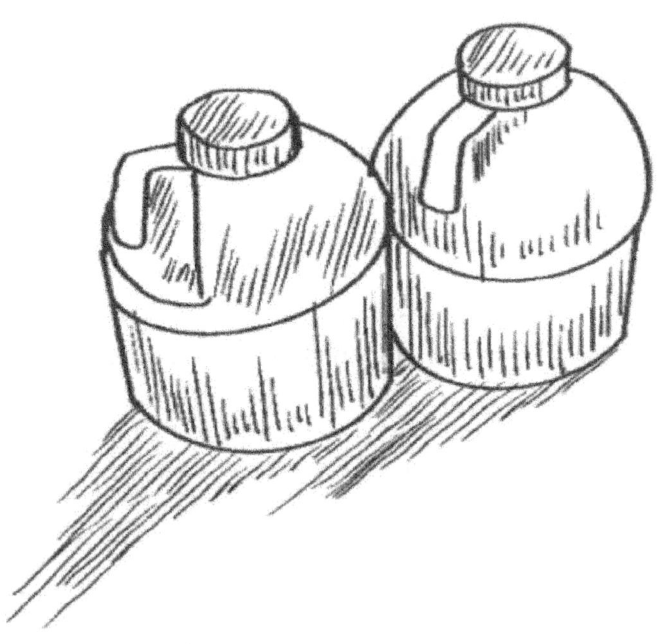

- If you can, leave your table covered but in the sun because if the table is warm, it will aid in self-leveling.

- Keep your blow torch near because epoxy for table tops is subject to more micro bubbles. So, after spreading the epoxy make sure to pop any bubbles. (**Tip**: Use a notched epoxy spreader). If you want you can opt to finish your project with varnish or polyurethane (not recommended because they finish with a yellowish hue).

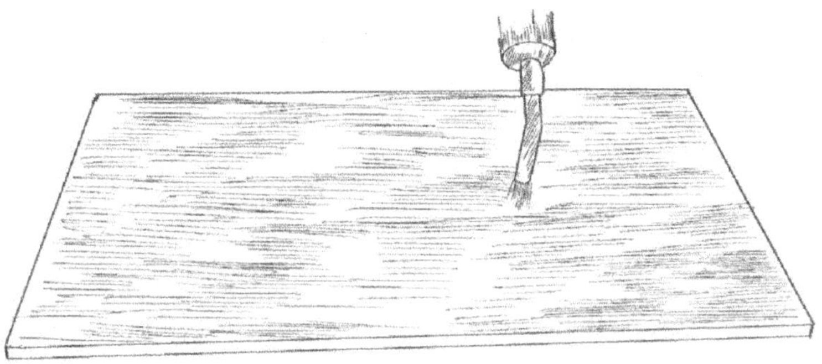

- Optional: If there is dust in your top coat after it is dry you can wet sand it with 800-grit sandpaper and then buff out the scratches. This is avoidable if you are extremely careful when applying your top coat. Make sure your room is clear of dust and drafts.

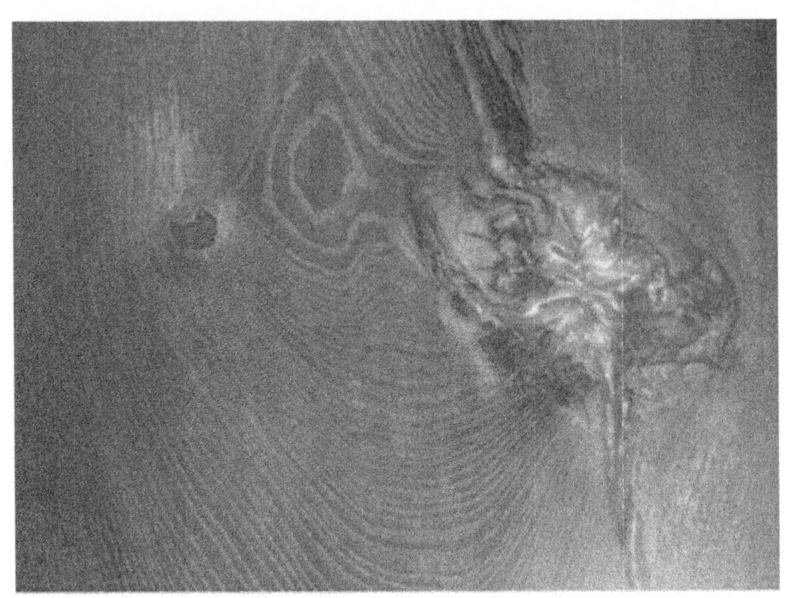

shutterstock.com • 1081083461

2-Sided Tapered Table legs

- Using the same wood as the table or wood you intend to finish similarly to the table making sure the wood is free of defects, straight, and square.

- On the blank wood draw the layout of your table leg.

- You can use a table saw, or better yet, a simple fixture jig and a band saw.

- Cut a 10-inch wide piece of plywood with your saw, making it three inches longer than the table leg and set the fence of the saw there.

- With the part that is going to be removed hanging off the edge, put your table leg plank on the jig.

- Mark the jog with the leg planks setting.

- Remove the plank and glue setting cleats on the edge that is long and at the end closest to you.

- Put the leg plank on the jig and cut.

- Rotate your plank by ¼ and finish cutting your leg.

- Sand off the band saw marks with sandpaper of a hand plane.

- Decide how you want to detail your edges.

- Sand the feet of your legs and apply finish to protect them from chipping. Also, sand out any transition marks, etc. (see image below

- Put your table on top of the legs.

- Now your table is ready to use!

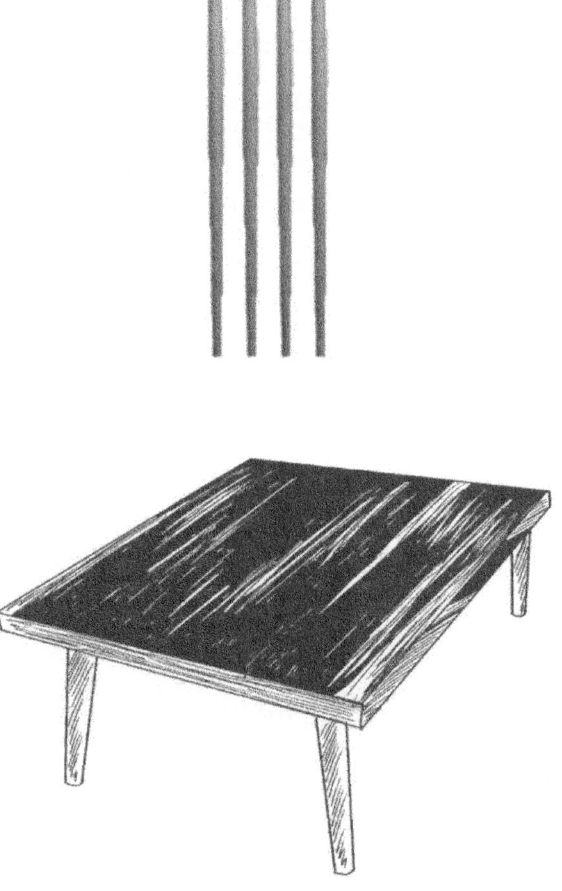

Chapter 7: Cougar Wood Burning Project

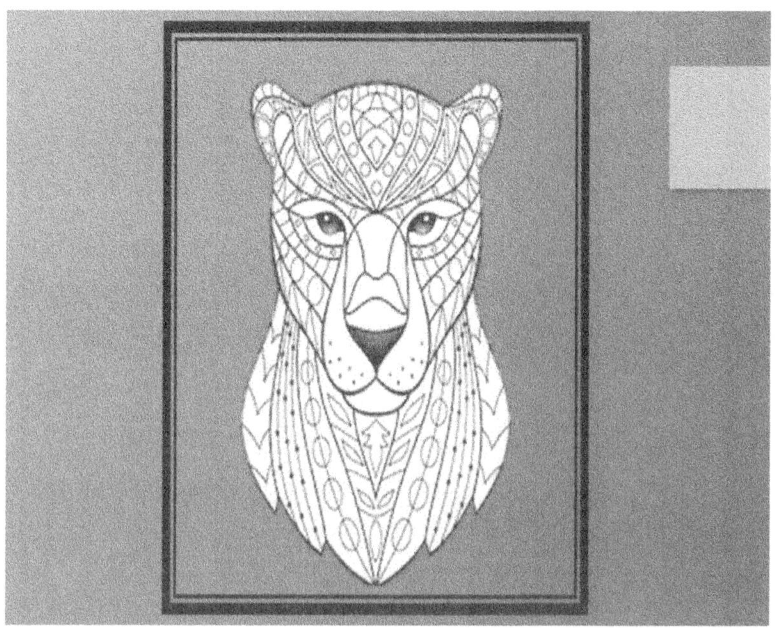

Materials

- Wood burning tool with varying temperature control

- Writing tip

- ⅛ inch thick and 12 inch square birch plywood

- #2 and #4 soft pencil

- 320-grit sandpaper

- Eraser, white

- V-gouge carving tool

- Leather strip for sharpening and honing compound

- Spray sealer acrylic

Steps

- The face of the cougar is a work of very fine lines. Each line is burned in the direction of the facial curves. How you set your burner temperature will determine your tonal values.

- Using 320-grit sandpaper, lightly sand your wood going in the direction of the grain as to avoid scratches.

- With a dry cloth, wipe the surface to remove any dust from sanding.

- With your #4 soft pencil, rub your patterned paper on the back and coat the whole surface.

- Tape your design on your wood, face up, with the cougar face down on the wood.

- Using a normal ink pen trace your pattern along the outline of the design.

- Remove the paper and you should have a gray graphite pattern.

- Set your pen on medium to hot and use your writing tip to start burning around the eyes, along the cheek and nose.

- Follow your pattern using your touch and pull line stroke for the short areas.

- Use dot strokes to fill in the black parts of the eyes, nose, and dots on the design (See pattern above).

- Reburn any places that need strengthening.

- Double check of smooth, crisp, and solid areas around the eyes.

- Gently wipe your finished burn to remove any dust from the burn.

- Use the white eraser to clean the whole piece's surface, erasing with the grain and then remove any eraser dust.

- Finish your project with three even, light coats of acrylic spray sealer.

Chapter 8: Pyrography Art on a Wooden Spatula

Make your kitchen full of art with your wood burning skills. You can start by making this wood burning spatula. Spatulas with unique designs can be used in your kitchen for both decorative and utility purposes. Yes, you can cook with it!

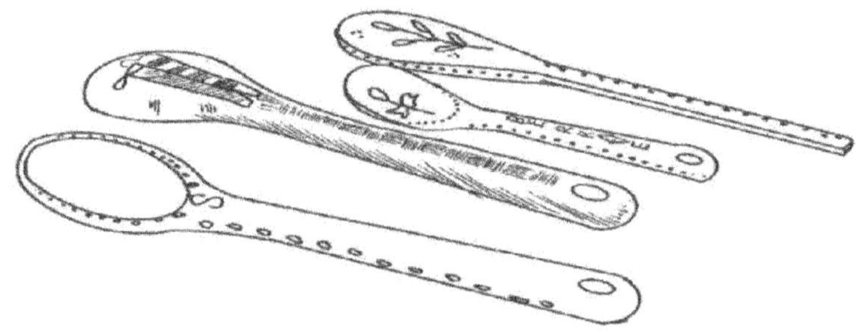

Materials

- A spatula of your size and liking

- 200- & 400-grit sanding paper

- Tung/Danish oil

- Wood burning tool

- Spear tip and flat shew tip for the wood burner

- Oiling brush

Steps

- Sand the spatula properly with the 200-grit sanding paper.

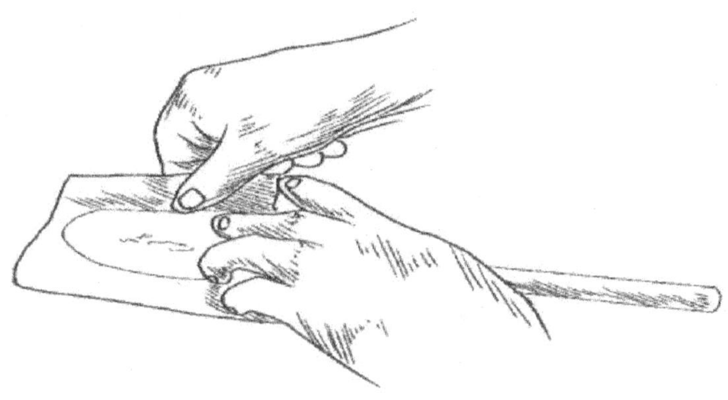

- Draw your preferred design on the spatula with a pencil or a stencil. See below for some patterns you can print and use if you desire.

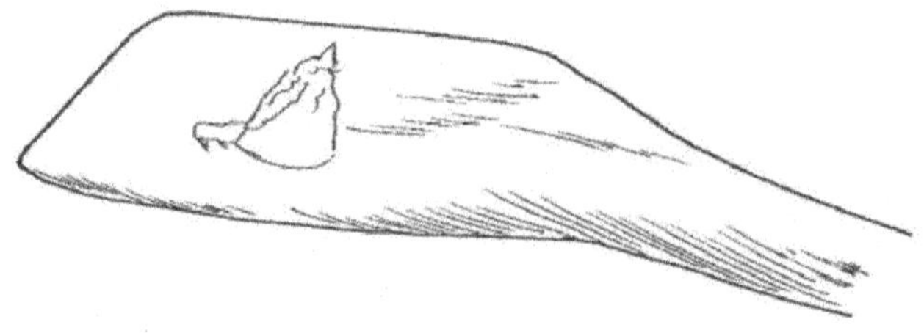

- Use your wood burner with the spear tip to draw the outline of your design.

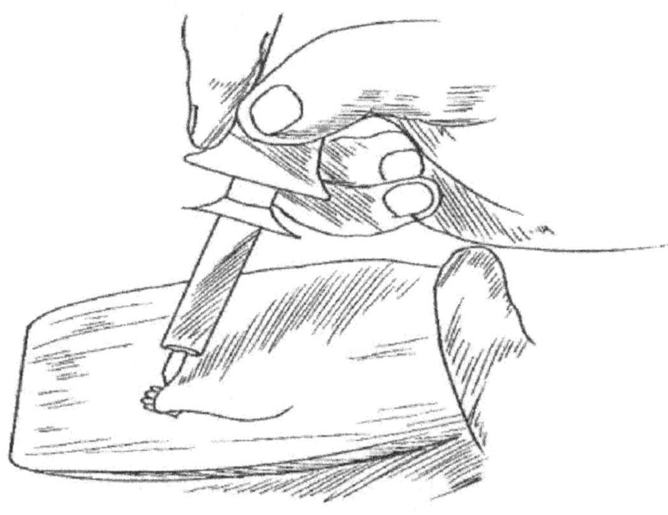

- Then use your flat shew tip for the detailing.

- Then use a 400-grit sanding paper for removing extra char formed.

- At last apply some Tung/Danish oil to secure your pyro-art.

Put your main focus on finishing the details of your first design and then see how many different designs you can make.

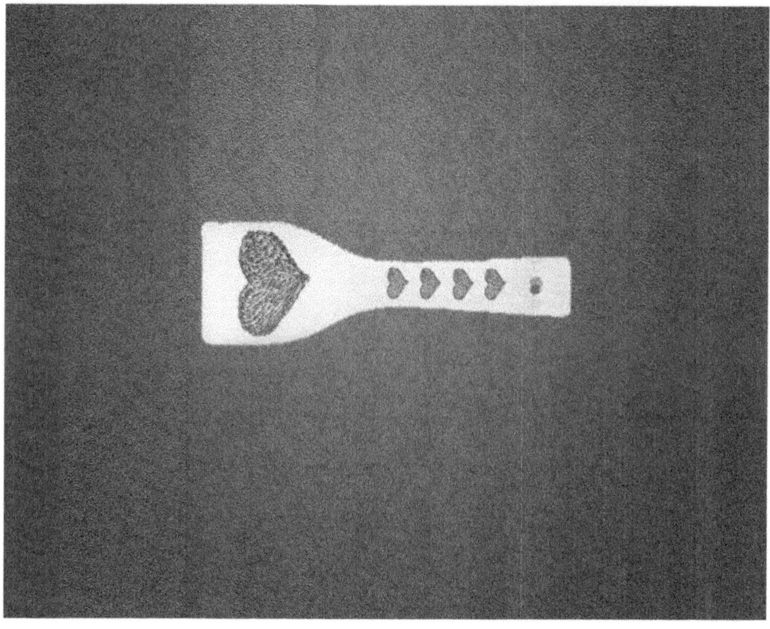

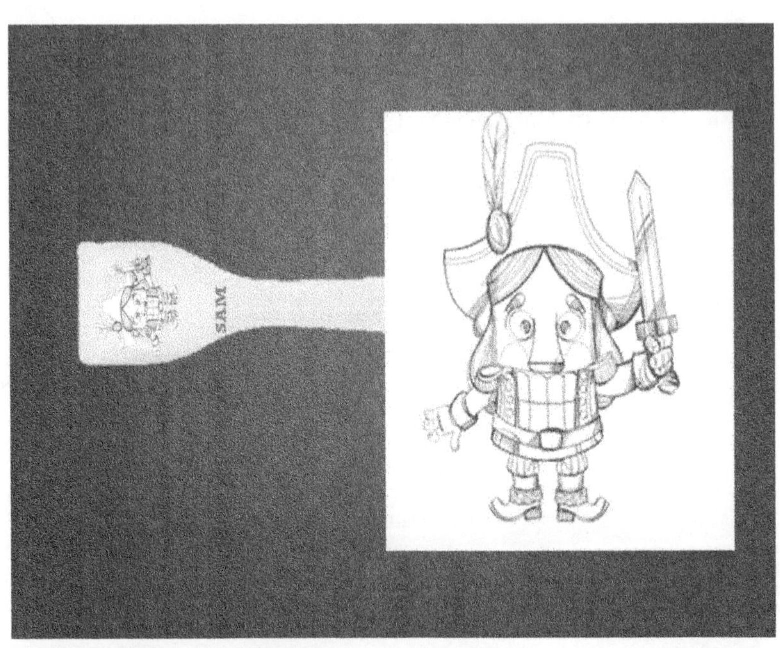
SAM

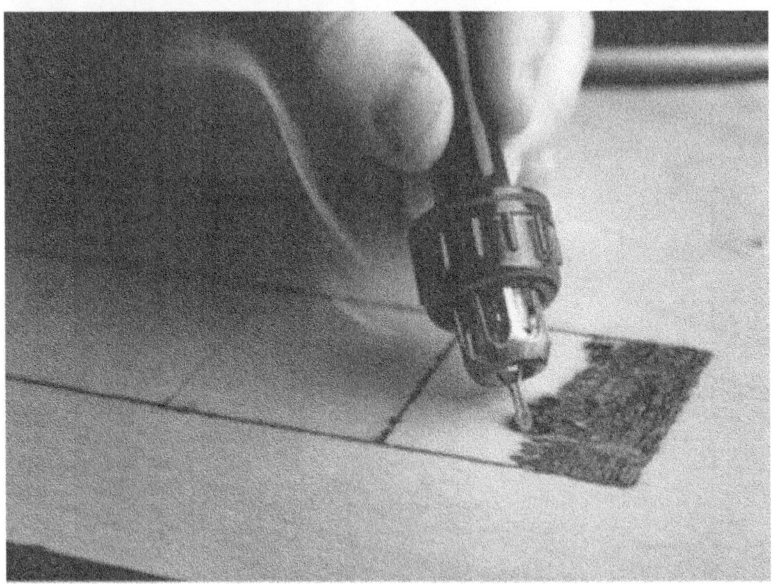
shutterstock.com • 1607229145

shutterstock.com • 601039193

Chapter 9: Superhero Pyrography Portraits

Pyrography portraits can give any room a special touch and show honor to your favorite superhero. They also make great gifts. No one has to sit still for hours either, today you can wood burn using a photo as a template. Brighten up any room with this woodcraft wall art. It is ideal for all superhero enthusiasts. These fun portraits have a positive impact on people and our planet. Make that unique, unexpected gift for that person who already has everything. With this project you can make amazing portraits using wood burning pyrography art. This project will mainly focus on making superhero portraits just because they are cool (see examples below).

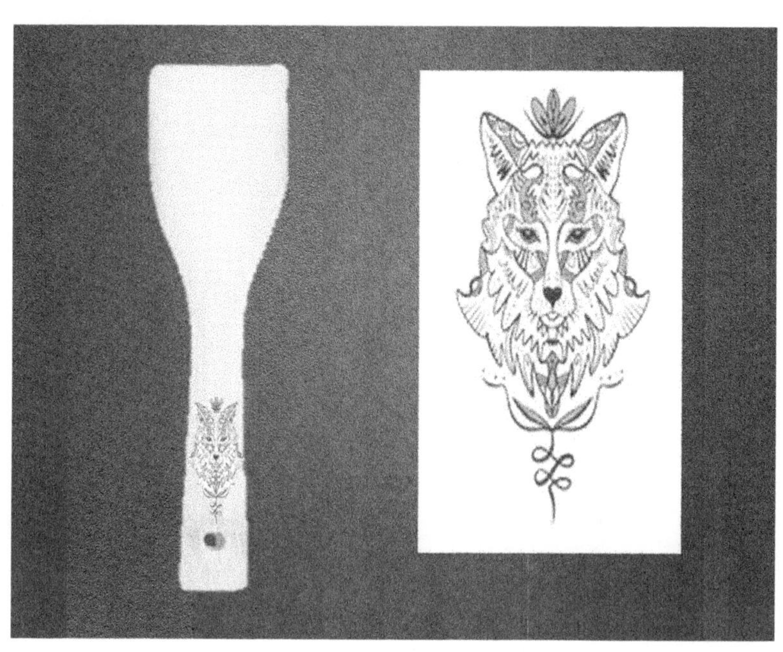

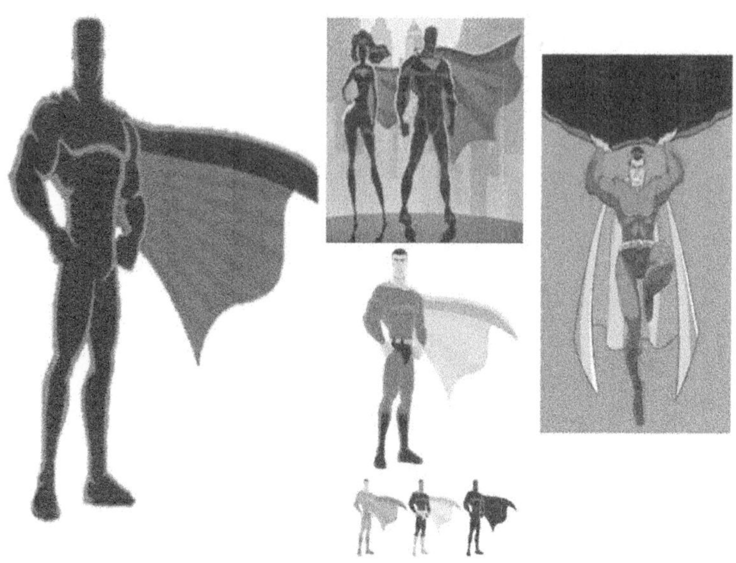

Materials

- A maple wood ply

- 800-grit sanding paper

- Wood burning tool

- Spear tip for your wood burning tool

- Pencil and stencil for your design

- Cotton pads

- Tung/Danish oil

- 00 and 7 size brush

- Oil brush

- Acrylic colors

Steps

- Use 800-grit sandpaper to smoothen your maple wood ply.

- Cut out a piece of transfer paper making it the same size as the image.

- Use your stencil and pencil to make an outline of your hero design.

- You can also use a printout and tracing paper to print the design on your wood.

- Once you have picked the image you want, print it to a size that fits on your piece of timber.

- You can write "boom" or "pow" on the back for a test.

- Make your burner hot so you can have brief contact with hardly any pressure. If it wasn't long enough, you can do it again. Check your results as you go along.

- With the graphite side down, tape the transfer paper to your piece of wood.

- Tape your transfer paper on the wood with your image over top.

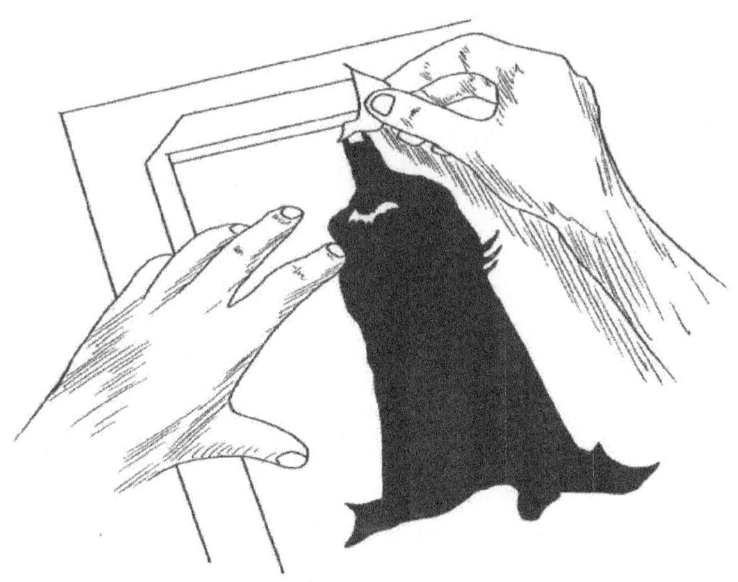

- Trace over your superhero with a little more pressure than normal to be sure to get a full transfer.

- When tracing over your superhero, you'll notice it's a little bit more difficult than simple objects. You have to pick the lines you want to trace over, which is an important step when you have to structure the face. Some of the trace patterns will be shadows not lines so be careful.

- Use your wood burner with a spear tip to make an outline of design.

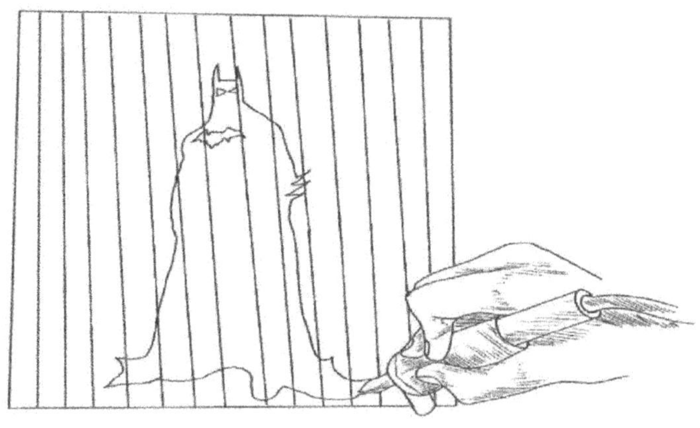

- When you think you have traced over all of the lines, remove the paper.

- Now use your cotton pads to fill colors in the background (preferably dark background).

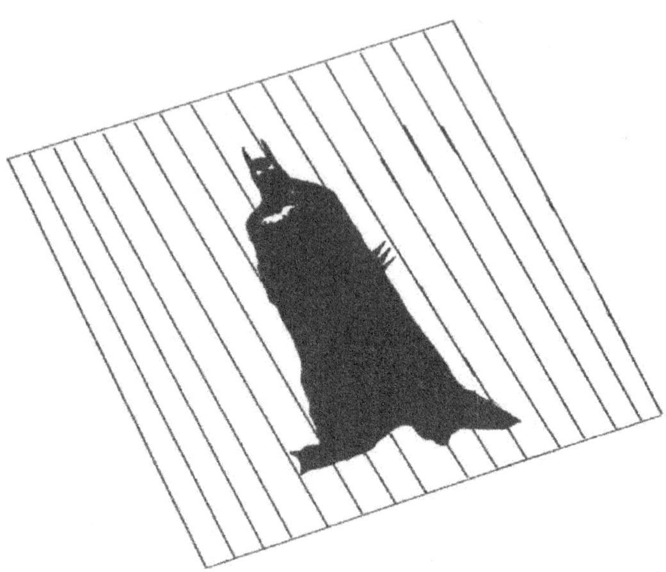

- Now start filling the details inside your design.

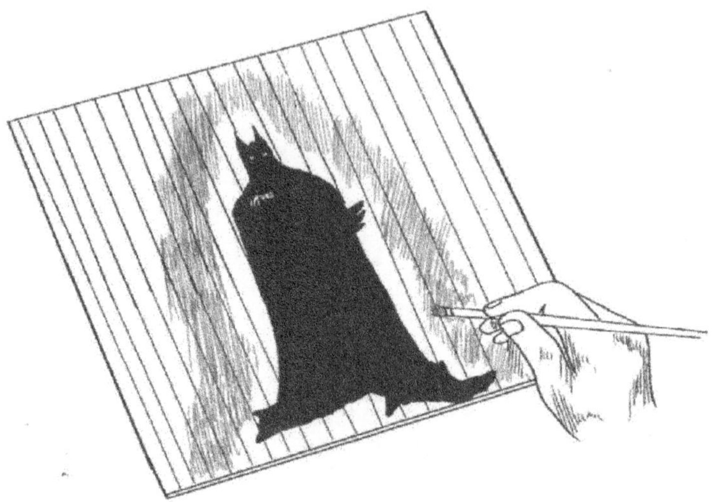

- Now after the detailing is done focus on the colors again to see that they spread evenly.

  - OR if you are shading, use light quick strokes, barefly brushing the piece, sliding your burner over the wood.

- Let it dry for at least 1 hour.

- Then apply your Tung/Danish oil with your oil brush onto your maple wood ply and let it dry.

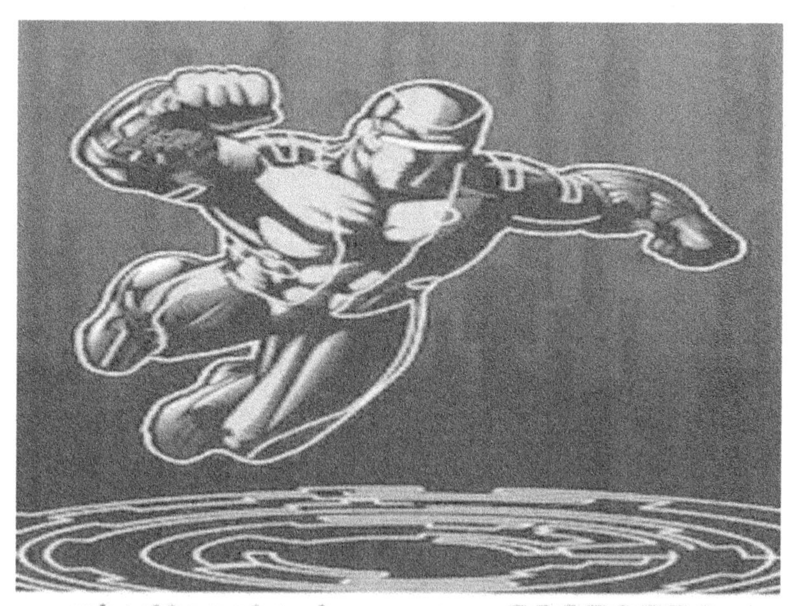

shutterstock.com • 68039020

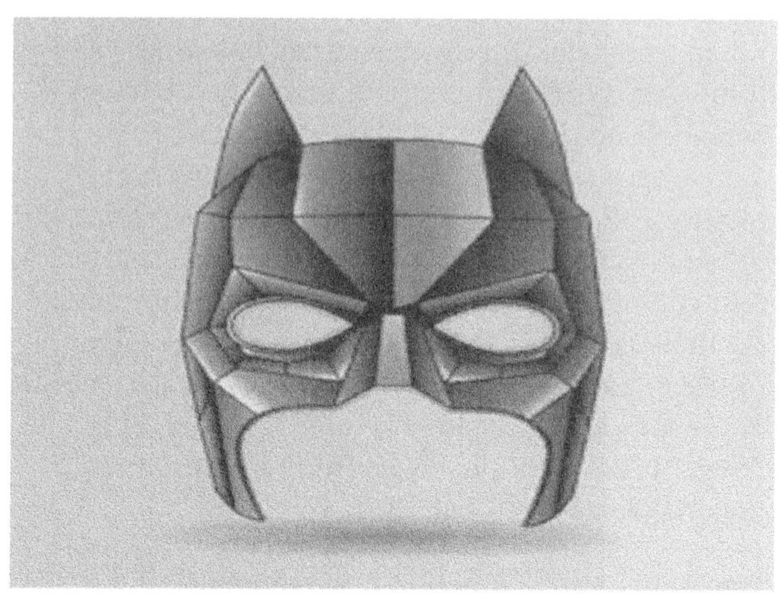

shutterstock.com • 675162490

Chapter 10:
Rustic Wood Tree Ornaments

Handcrafted, wood burned tree ornaments can be a total joy to make during the holidays. Start a collection that can be passed down through generations, or give one as a gift that will have your signature or special message on it. For so many reasons, burning your own tree ornaments is beneficial to you, your family, and your home. It is a great way to create family bonds and cherished memories. This project may take some patience and effort, but when finished everyone will be proud to have a place on the tree for their special ornament. When complete, you can keep them stored for years to come. A gift of a handcrafted Christmas ornament is personal and timeless. It is like giving a piece of nature back to the tree. Creating traditions to carry on each year brings families together. Burning the ornaments in this project and then seeing them every year will be a great tradition. Another thing to think about is the money that can be saved from making things at home. Getting creative with your pyrography ornaments can really help keep the holiday costs down. It is all about having a wonderful time and making memories for all those you love.

Materials

- Basswood rounds

- Wood burning kit

- Stamp designs (if you do not want to freehand)

- Ink pad (brown)

- Ribbon color of your choice

- Pinecones

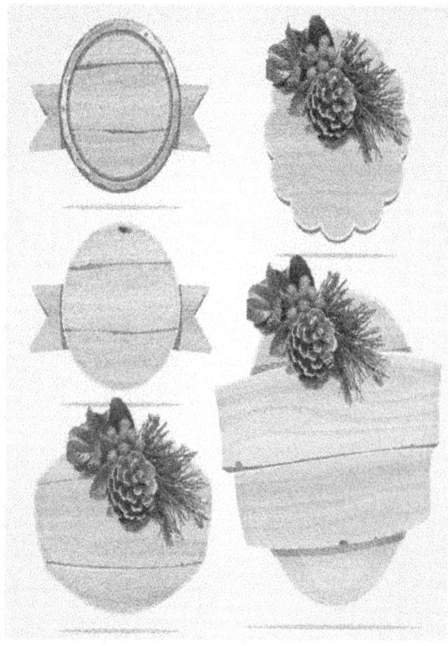

Steps

- Preheat your tool for at least 15 minutes.

- Place your stamp in the center of the ornament.

- Using light pressure outline your image.

- Burn a name or greeting on the back

- Take two small pinecones and with the ribbon attach them to the top of the ornament so they are perched on top as an extra decorative element.

- You can also use these as coasters!

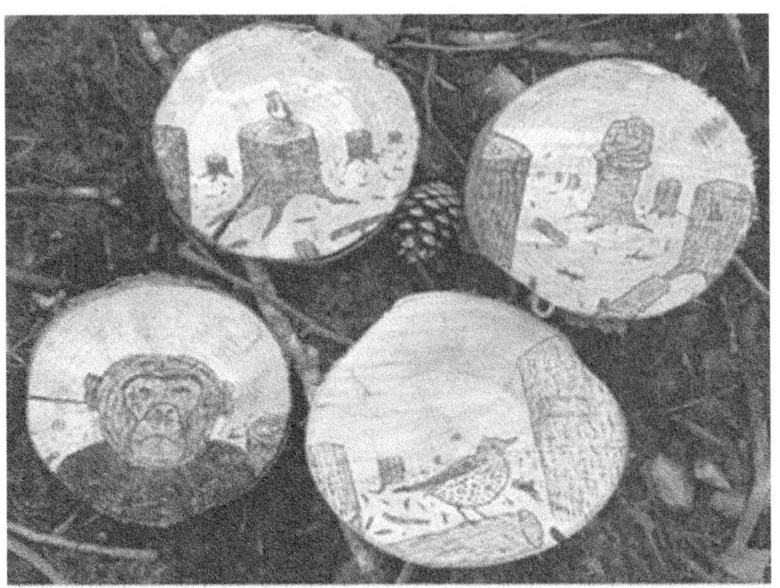

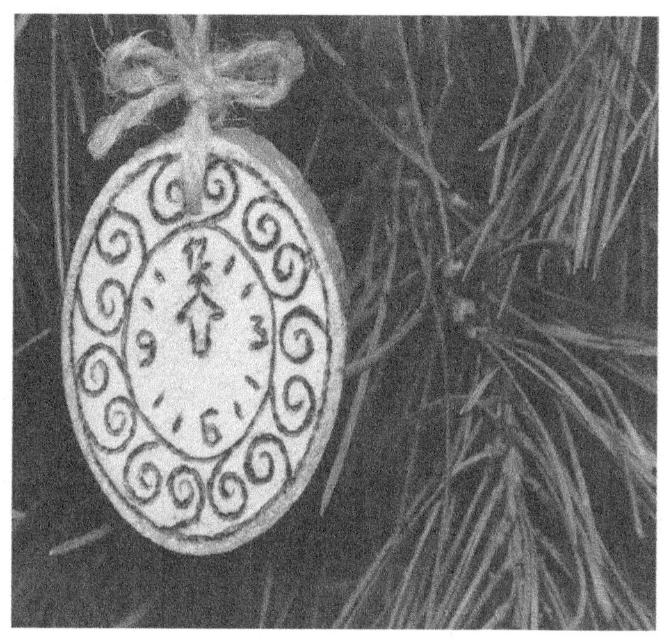

With the skills you have learned in this book, as a future project, special handcrafted ornaments that contain the images of a family member is something you can make to really add a personal touch for someone you love. Everyone you know will want you to make one for them. They will be inspired by the silhouette artistry you made. Your cuts will be interpretations from silhouettes from sketching the outline of someone you want to craft for. All you would need to do for this art form is use a digital camera, computer, and scroll saw. You will surely be able to come up with something that is well within your artistic abilities, and not too difficult to produce.

How To Make Silhouette Ornaments

Take a few profile pictures of the person you want to feature (see image below). You have to get a clean picture so you can outline the details. Print out the picture and cut it into the circle size of your ornament (leave ⅛ inch border). Draw a circle around the silhouette. Trace the silhouette on tracing paper with graphite pencil. You can even make the eyelashes exaggerated to add personality to the ornament. Plump up the lower lip and darken the neck line (it may take a couple of tries). If you want you can use photo software to modify your photo. Burn the outline of the silhouette and use your favorite finish.

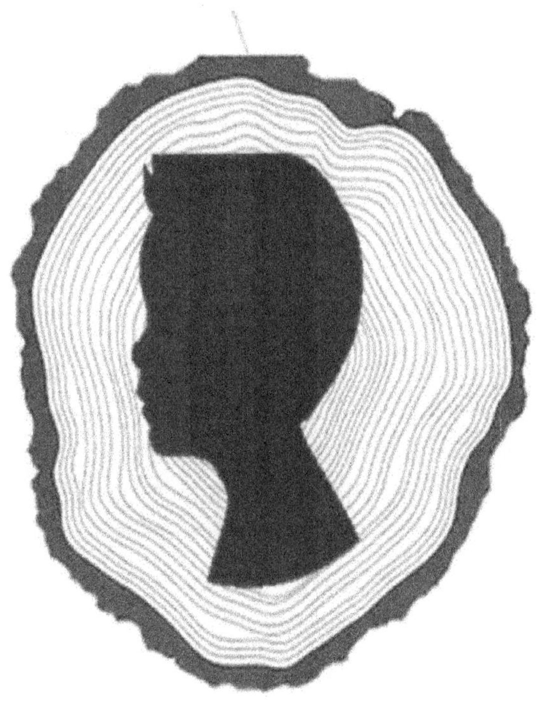

Chapter 11:
Wall Art

Unleash your creativeness by transforming any scrap wood or chosen timber pieces into beautiful art. Decorating your home or office with wall art burned and crafted by you projects deep meaning into anyone who views it. Wood is a natural canvas that comes with its own built in personality. Grains of different sizes and shapes, varying resin consistencies, and a wealth of hues can give the crafter different challenges with the result being a masterpiece of lasting artwork (see image below).

When moving into a new apartment or house there is always that second when you see a blank wall and your imagination runs wild with how to give it personality. As fun as it may seem to shop for wall art, creating it yourself gives you quality art at a reasonable price, and the satisfaction of knowing where it came from. The whole family will enjoy seeing a work of handcrafted wood burned art and it will last forever. Walls are an essential part to the attraction of every room in your home. Having the best decor on the walls will increase the elegance and the style of the room while at the same time expressing your personality is a classic way.

This wall pyrography project will appear close to nature which is something everyone admires in a home. This rustic project is made of natural raw materials and therefore it is the best way to give that extra accent to your walls and elevate their elegance while you enjoy the satisfaction of having spent the time devoted to this endeavor. This project will ensure you and yours will remain connected to nature.

Materials

- 1 wood slice from any hobby store

- Wood burner kit

- A design you wish to use

- Pencil

- Sandpaper

Steps

- Print your design on a regular piece of copy paper. Think of memorable places or times in your life. Get creative.

- Flip over the paper and sketch the design with a pencil.

- Position and tape down the design with the right side up on the wood slice.

- Using medium pressure, go over your design with a pencil.

- After stenciling the entire design, use a rounded tip and start burning. If you have letters, trace the outline of them first and then fill them in.

- Carefully sand any mistakes away.

- Touch up any areas that seem too light.

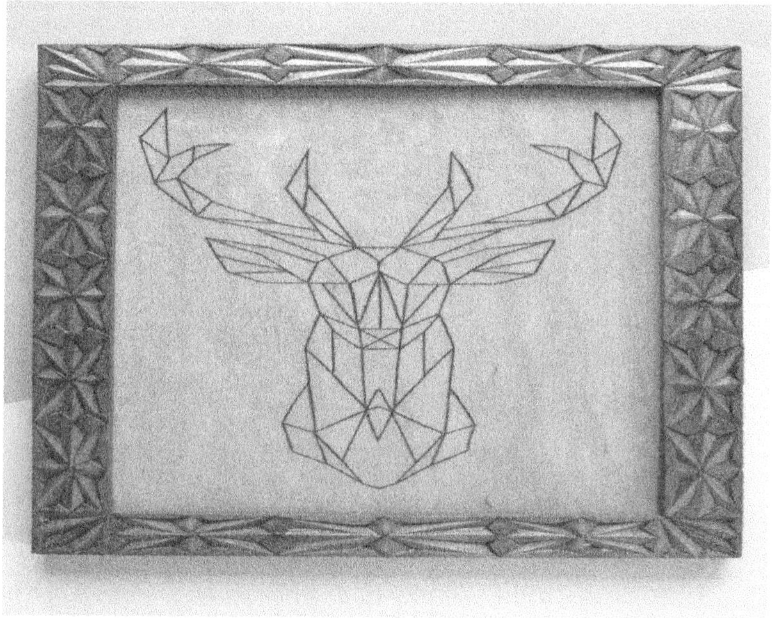

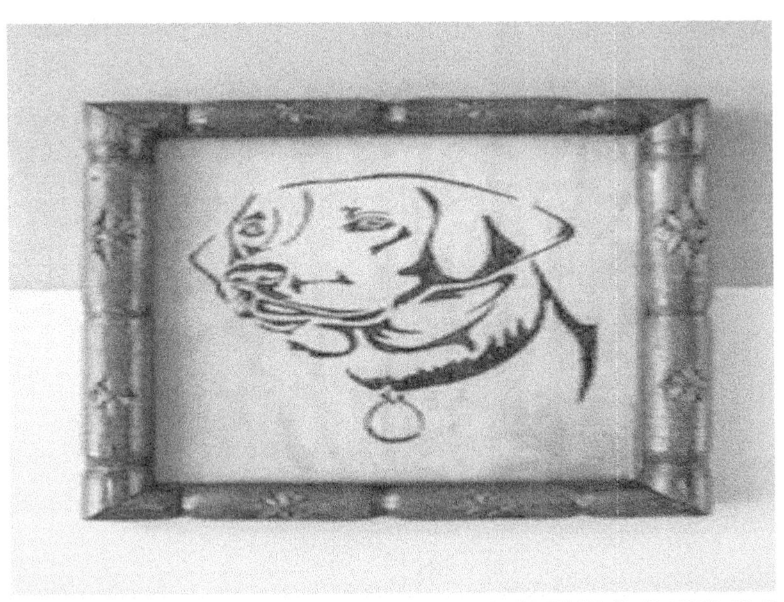

Chapter 12:
Wood Carving Board

What is a kitchen without a good quality carving board? One of the nicest things in a kitchen is a beautiful wooden cutting board. You can make one that will be a central feature in your kitchen.

Some people use plastic cutting boards which are not very attractive and not that healthy. A study published by the University of Wisconsin discussed that every time a knife is used on a plastic board, it leaves a tiny cut that makes a suitable home for bacteria to thrive in (Ak, Cliver, & Kaspar, 1994). Plastic cutting boards are also not very eco-friendly.

Crafting and burning your own carving board will delight you, your family, and your guests for now and for generations to come. Crafting your own carving board can be done with two different types of surfaces; edge grain or end grain. This is important to consider because both surfaces of the cutting board have an effect on knives. With an edge-grain carving board's surface, it will look kind of like the side of a 2 by 4. So, the best selection is a board with edge-grain surface so you can see the gorgeous cherry or maple finish on the surface as you're cutting (see image below). Using hardwoods such as oak or maple will not scar as easily as plastic or softwoods. Then again, softwoods will not dull your knives as quickly as hardwoods.

In the steps below there are suggested types of wood that are best for this project. Beechwood and maple do not end up with knife slits where bacteria can grow. They are also easier on your knife blades. Either type of board edge-grain or end-grain are long lasting and sanitary. (**Tip**: Wood is porous and meat juices are susceptible to growing bacteria, so use antibacterial wipes or soapy water to clean your board when finished. Don't use chlorine based products because it can damage the wood.) Let your board dry completely before storing it so it will not warp. You probably won't want to store it anyway because you will also want to use it as decor. Unlike plastic, wooden cutting boards don't need to be thrown out when they get cuts. Just sand the surface down with a fine-grit sandpaper, wash it, dry it and then rub it down with a bit of mineral oil. It'll be good as new.

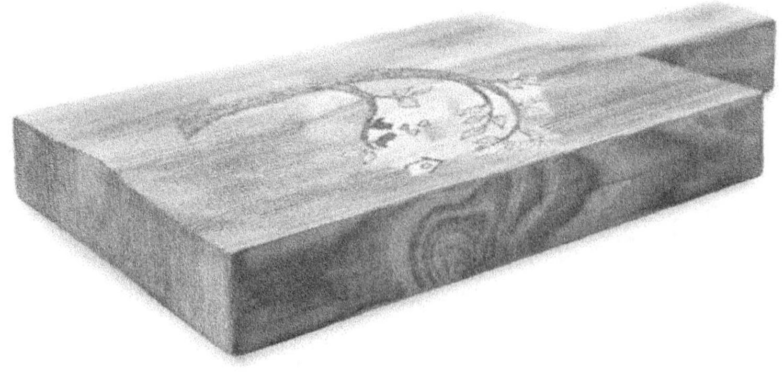

Materials

- 1 x 12 inch x 16 inches wood board (see step by step instruction below)

- Sandpaper

- Router

- Handsaw

- Alphabet bits

- Stamps

- Glue

Steps

- Wood board: Dense hardwood timber such as cherry, maple, or walnut is the best wood for carving boards. Dense hardwood has a closed grain, which is nice, but make sure it is not warped, has knots, and is flat. Use end-grain wood if possible (End grain is when the wood grains are not parallel but perpendicular to the cutting surface).

  - Mark a measured 1 x 12 inch board at 16 inches

  - Use a hand saw and cut the wood. Cut wood on the line using a hand saw.

- The dimensions for your carving board will be 1 x 12 x 16 inches.

- Handle

  - Mark a measure 1 ½ inches from the corners on each side (should look like a plus sign +)

  - With a ⅝ inch drill bit, drill a hole through the plank where you marked it.

  - On both sides and using 220-grit sandpaper and sanding block, sand each edge.

  - Use your sanding block to round the corners.

  - Wrap sandpaper around a dowel and sand the inside of the handle.

  - If you want it to look professional, round the edges with a router using a chamfer bit.

  - Use a damp cloth and wipe away any sawdust.

- Using the shading point and with light pressure sketch three or four flowering lines on both sides of the board.

- When your pen is hot enough use the edge of the shading point to burn over the flowering lines.

- Then erase the pencil.

- Using the large flat area on your shading point burn the leaves onto the flowering lines.

- Trace a circle around a bowl either on the top, bottom, or center. Trace over the circle adding leaves. Burn the circle and leaves.

- Using food grade mineral oil, polish your wood, wipe clean, and buff.

Chapter 13:
Twig Earrings

Have you ever been in a unique shop, seen the most adorable wooden earrings but they were a bit too pricey to buy? Here is the good news. You can not only make your own earrings but you can style them to accent any apparel, season, or special event. They will be fabulous and fun to make for a fraction of the cost you would pay in those fancy shops. Also, they are customized by your creative imagination.

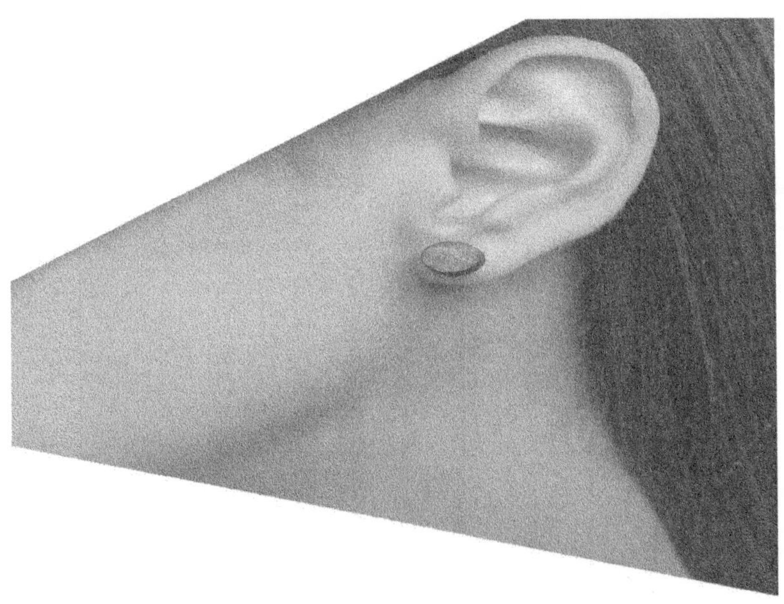

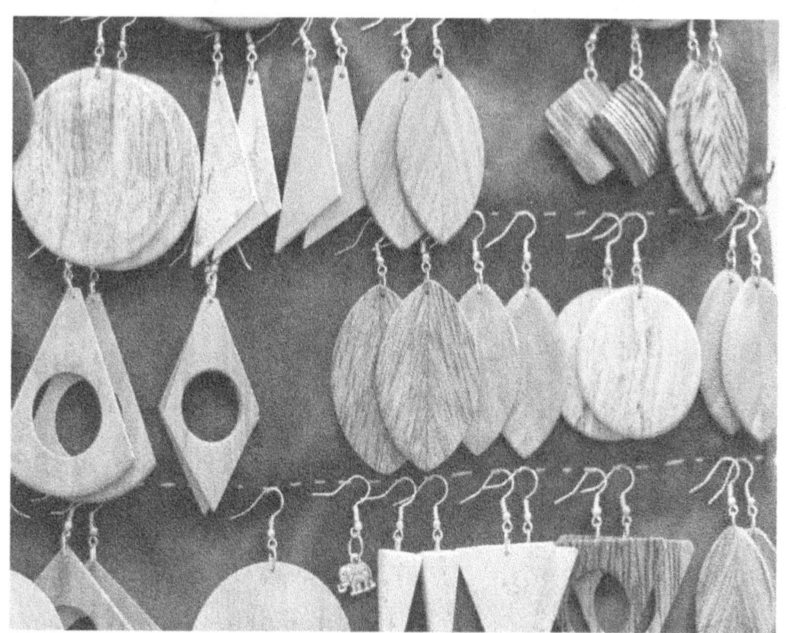

Take a look in your backyard or at a park and you'll be surprised how many beautiful wooden pieces will seem like they were placed there just for you to bring home, burn and make your own. They also are just right for party giveaways, bridal shower gifts, and birthdays. Make sure to use your special ingredient. That, of course, is TLC - tender, loving, care.

Materials

- Branches

- Hand saw

- Wood burning kit

- Earring hooks

- Cleaning alcohol

- Glue

- Thin wire

- Small pliers

- Aluminum foil

Steps

- First you want to sanitize the earring hooks.

- Select a few twigs and slice small rounds with your hand saw.

- Burn a tiny hole at the top of each circular piece.

- With your wood burning tool burn any elegant or playful design your creative mind comes up with. Beware, this is time consuming because the pieces are so small.

- Cut two pieces of wire 2 ½ inches long. Using pliers cut the wire into two pieces for the earrings. This part of the wire hangs off the hooks and is attached to the earrings. You can make them as dangly as you want or even easily curl up one end of the wire until it is almost a circle (curves back toward itself).

- Run a piece of wire through each earring and attach the wood. Holding the curled piece of the wire, run it through the twig earring. Curl it all the way around the hole at the top of the earring so that it is connected together.

- For stud earrings, don't use the hooks. Just use epoxy glue to attach the metal posts to the back of the wood pieces.

Chapter 14:
Picture Frame

So many of us have a tough time giving something unique for Mother's Day or Father's Day. You can't give a goofy pair of socks or a new apron every year! Some people buy what they want for themselves, so the only way to remedy this issue is to craft it yourself! Buying a picture frame can be costly, but with the following project, your frames will look like they cost a fortune and yet they will be priceless as they are passed down through generations.

Making a picture frame is very rewarding. The key to a successful cut in this project is not just correctly mitering the corner cuts, but being certain the opposite ends of the frame are exactly the same lengths. There will be a gap in the corner if not cut correctly. Often people think they have a gap because the miter angle is off, but it is more likely that the frame lengths were not quite correct.

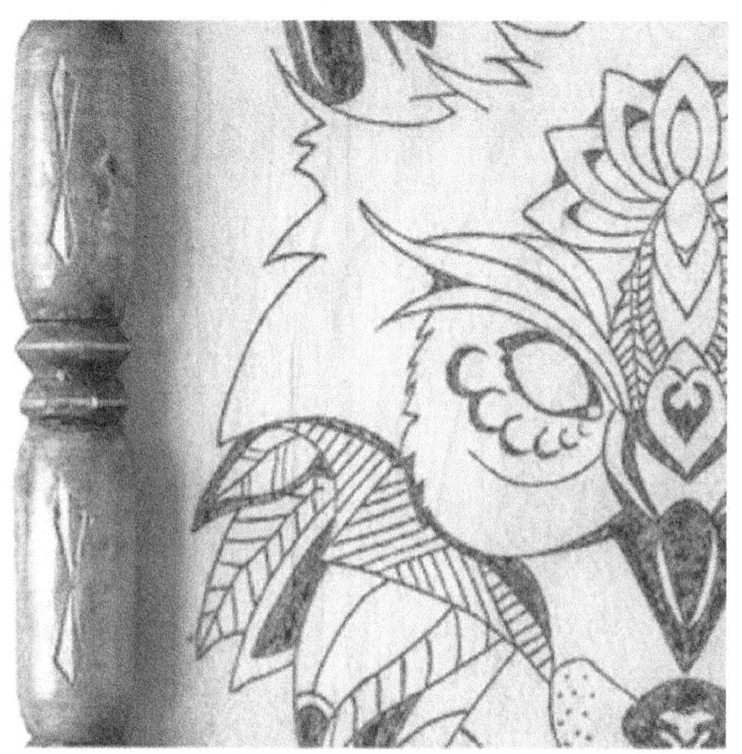

shutterstock.com • 1694854114

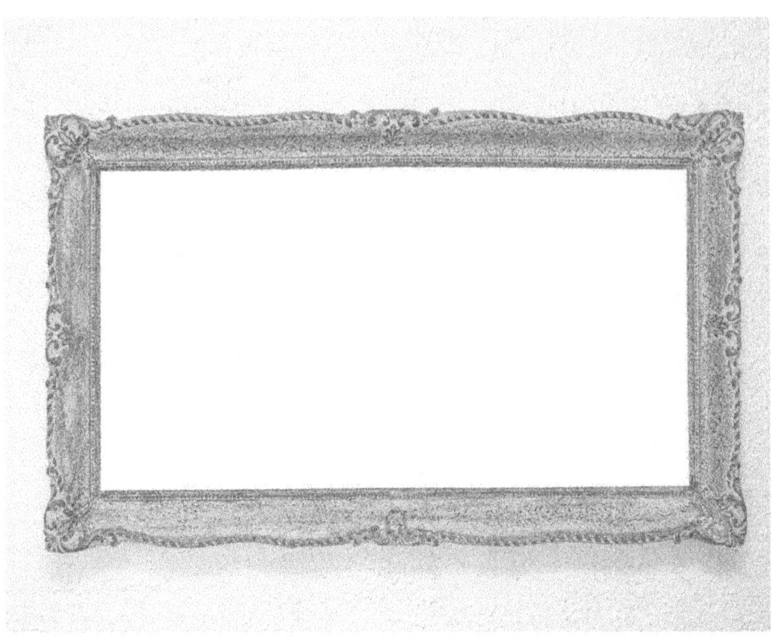

Materials

- 1 x 4 board(s) (the size depends on what you want to frame but dimensions are added here as a reference)

- Wood burning kit

- Stain

- Sandpaper

- Dowels

- Dowel jig

- Clamps

- Drill

- Wood glue

- Miter saw

- Router

- Router bit

- Rabbeting bit

- Chisel

- Glass panel

- Picture mat

- Exacto knife

- Picture frame tabs

Steps

- Figure out the size of your frame by having the picture measured and knowing the width of the matting you want around the picture.

  - Here is the formula: {Width (***equals***) the width of the picture (***plus***) 2 times width of the mat (***plus***) 2 times with width of the frame (***minus***) ¾ inches}.

- To figure how much wood you need to make the frame and using the above formula, it is 2 times the height from above and 2 times the width from the formula above.

- Make a 3-inch-wide mat on all sides of the picture.

- Make your frame 2 ¾ inches wide on each side. To determine how much wood you need for the frame, take 2 x height from above + 2 x width from above.

- Using a miter saw, cut down the plank to just over the width and length you calculated from Steps 1 and 2.

- Saw off on edge with a table saw and then separate the plank in two to have (2) 2 ¾ inch wide pieces.

- If you have decided you are going to use a 1x wood plank begin with the following: Adjust your miter angle to 45 degrees and saw 2 pieces (with miters, NOT parallel, so your length is equal to the width you calculated in Step 1. Then saw 2 pieces in the same manner, with the length equal to the height from Step 1.

- Sand all of the boards now because it is easier than when they are assembled.

- Using a ⅜ inch dowel jig, drill ¾ inch deep dowel holes into each corner.

- You have corresponding holes when you drill so they line-up perfectly with the frame.

- Line the edge of your jig on each piece on the inside corner of the miter and then you can clamp it into place for drilling the holes.

- **Make sure your jig is lined up in the same place on each piece of your frame.

- If you can get a second set of hands for this step it would be helpful. Put glue on one corner at a time. Then apply the glue into the holes and each miter and insert the dowels.

- Once all your holes are drilled on each end of each piece, it's time to apply the glue.

- As best as you can, squeeze them together beginning on one corner and making your way around.

- Once you have your dowels started in place, use clamps to help you make your frame good and square. Once the glue is completely dry, sand the corners to rid them of any glue that squeezed through during assembly.

- Time to get ready to burn!

- Heat up your woodburner for at least 5 minutes.

- Practice on a piece of scrap before you start working on the frame.

- Using a pencil and a ruler lightly mark where your design is going to be on your frame.

- If your design has a lot of detail, take your time. You might want to use stamps or stencils.

- After burning and smiling about your accomplishment, erase any pencil marks and sand your frame with fine-grit sandpaper to make it smooth.

- Stain, varnish, or leave it natural.

Get creative! You can burn any of these designs below, or design your own.

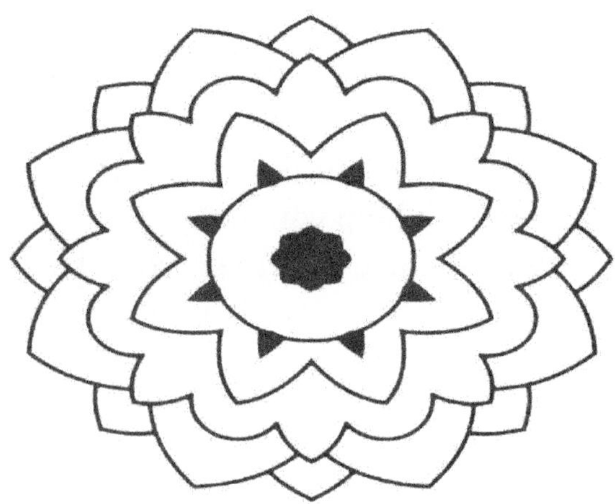

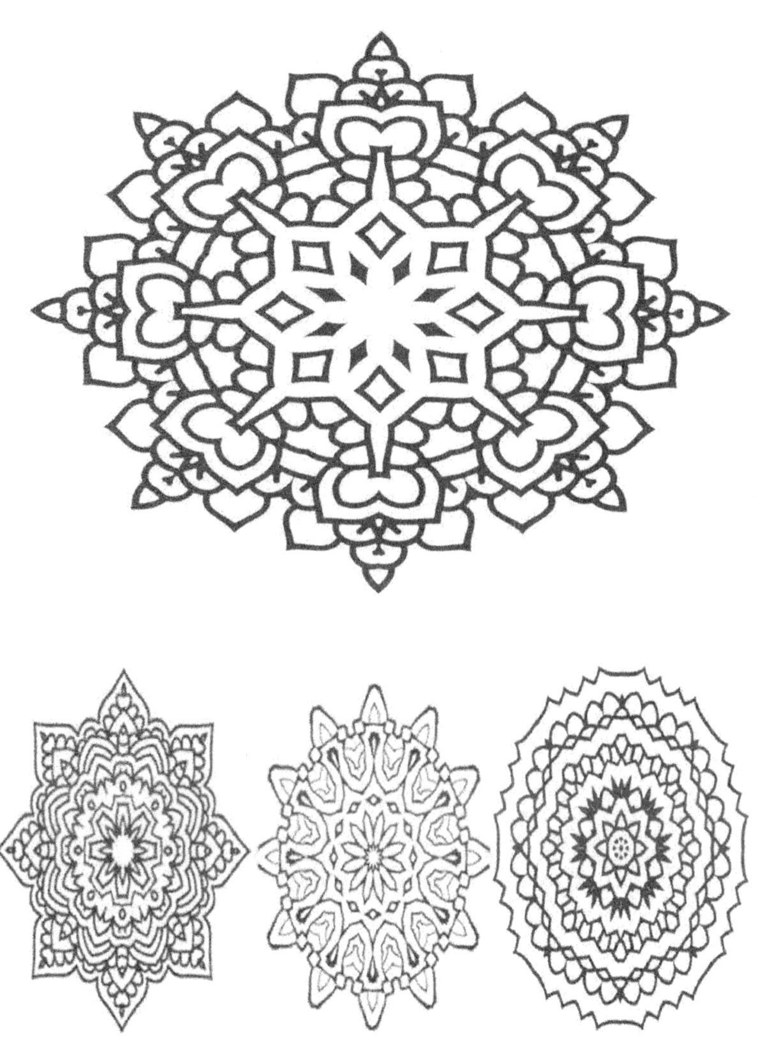

Chapter 15:
Personalized Clothes Hangers

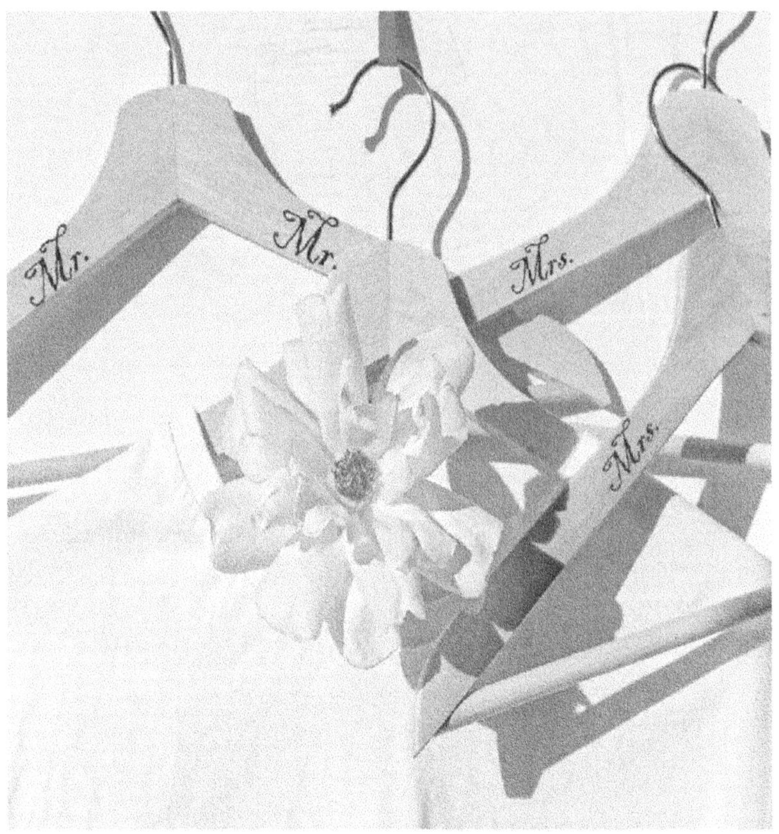

These woodburned hangers can make fantastic gifts. They add such a special touch to any closet, make great conversation pieces (especially when burned with a His or Hers). Handcrafted for a bride and groom, these are a wonderful accessory for the "big" day. Personalized gifts always add a little something extra. Another fantastic idea is to add your business logo or company name to your hangers using your wood burning skills. They have a dual purpose: having a place for your employees to hang their coats, and as a great marketing tool, especially if you make them part of a give-away during a sale.

Get rid of your mismatched plastic hangers because wooden hangers are an upgrade. If you do not live near your extended family and have a lot of overnight guests, woodburned personalized hangers will make them feel welcome. Simply buy some wooden hangers and sand them down to make them perfectly smooth. Dots are one of the easier designs or you can use the monogramming technique. Remember to get creative. Mark your design ahead of time with a pencil and erase after burning and before staining.

Steps

- Buy wooden hangers at any hobby store or superstore.

- Either print from your computer or buy letter stickers around ½ inch in size.

- Plan your spacing with a ruler.

- Plan where on the hangers you want your words.

- Use a pencil to outline your letters.

- After you outline your letters, peel them off of the hangers.

- Using your ball point tip, burn your design.

- Attach small bows to the top of each hanger (if gift giving).

Here are some suggested phrases:

- Home Sweet Home

- Smile

- mi casa es tu casa

- Bless this home

- Hanging out

- Rock n roll...is...here...to...stay (multiple hangers)

- I love you

- and the list goes on...

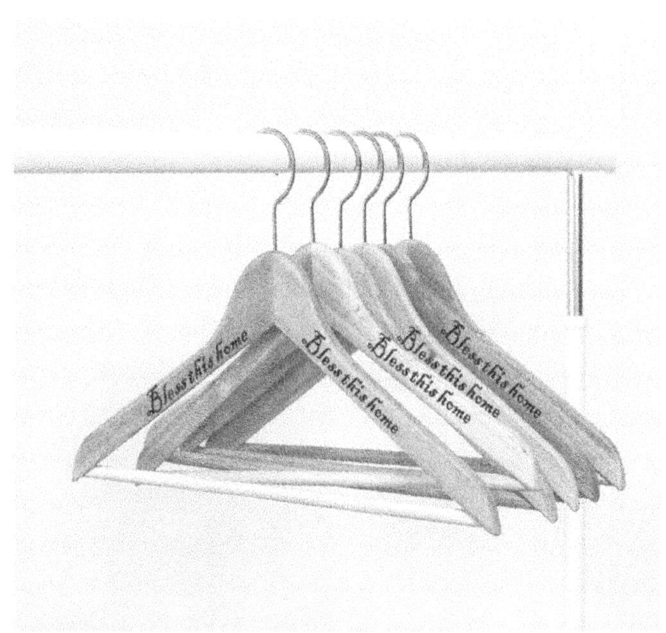

These personalized hangers are just perfect for a hall closet or a guest room. The ideas are practically endless. You can even make a personalized baby gift with child sized hangers. The options are endless.

Chapter 16:
Farmhouse Wooden Caddy

If you are tired of looking at loaves of bread, a box of crackers, and a jar of peanuts haphazardly laying atop of the fridge or counter, you will love this decorative caddy that you can make with your wood burning skills.

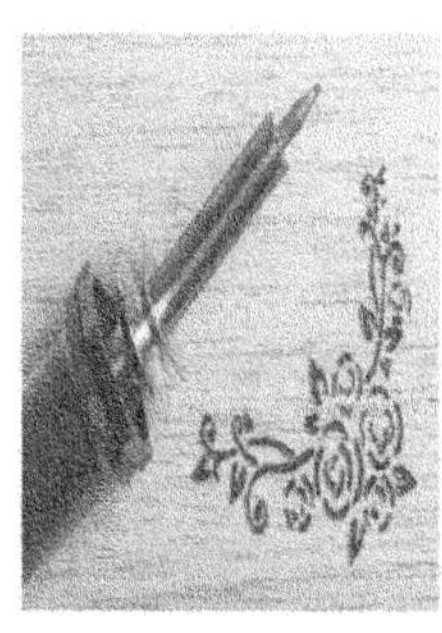 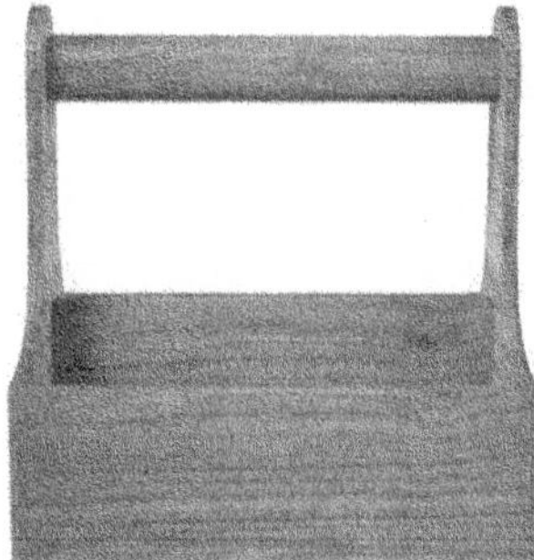 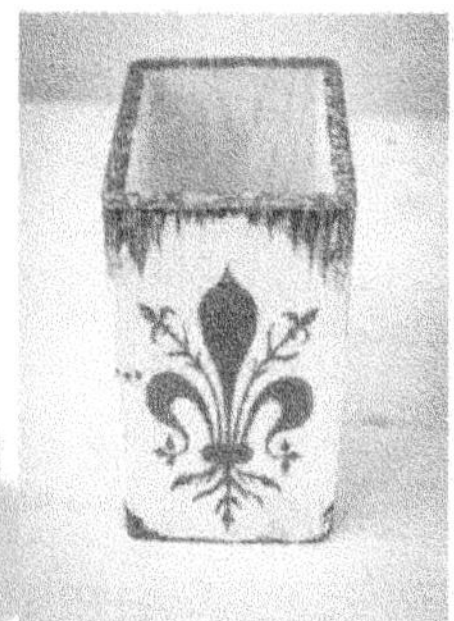

Materials

- Tape measure

- Miter saw

- Wood square

- Clamps

- Hammer and nails (or better yet a nail gun)

- Drill

- ⅞ of an inch bit (forstner)

  - A forstner bit drills a hole with a flat bottom. This way you will have the exact depth you need. These bits are led by a wide outside rim, not by the tip like most drill bits.

- 220- and 150-grit sandpaper

- Wood glue

- 1¼ inch 18 gauge brad nails

- Filler

- Stain

- Sealer

- Disposable brush (chippy brush) cuts

- 1 x 3 x 8 (one)

- 1 x 4 x 8 (one)

- 1 x 2 x 8 (one)

- ¾ inch 3 foot dowel

Cuts

- Two 1 x 3 cut 18 inches (long side of the caddy frame)

- Two 1 x 3 cut 7 ¼ inches (short side of the caddy frame)

- Two 1 x 4 cut 16.5 inches (the caddy bottom)

- Two 1 x 2 cut 13 inches (handle is attached to these vertical sides)

- ¾ inch dowel at 19 inches for the handle.

Steps

- Using the four pieces you cut from the 1 x 3, create the caddy frame, align the joints with a square and clamp them in place.

- Put wood glue on the edges and nail a short piece to a long piece until you have your frame.

- Nail the 1 x 4 wood pieces to the bottom inside of the frame to create the caddy bottom.

- Put in the 1 x 4 wood piece and then glue or nail it around the outside of the frame. It is best to nail it because it is the bottom and will hold whatever is in your caddy. Also, leave about a ¼ inch gap between the bottom boards.

- For the handle, use a pencil to mark the center point on the top of the 1 x 2 at ¾ inch from the top.

- With a ⅞ inch forstner bit, drill about ½ of an inch deep.

- Adhere one of the 1 x 2 to the frame using glue and nailing it into place.

- With the other 1 x 2 hold in place and measure from the inside of the holes you drilled so you can measure the dowel.

- Put wood glue in each 1 x 2 drilled hole and insert the dowel into the 1 x 2 that is already attached. (Once you are hands on this will make perfect sense).

- Attach the last 1 x 2.

- Sand the caddy after you fill the nail holes.

- Heat up your burner... IT'S TIME TO BURN!

- It is a personal choice how you want to burn your caddy (see examples at the beginning of this chapter).

- Burn and varnish.

Chapter 17: Wood Burned Vases

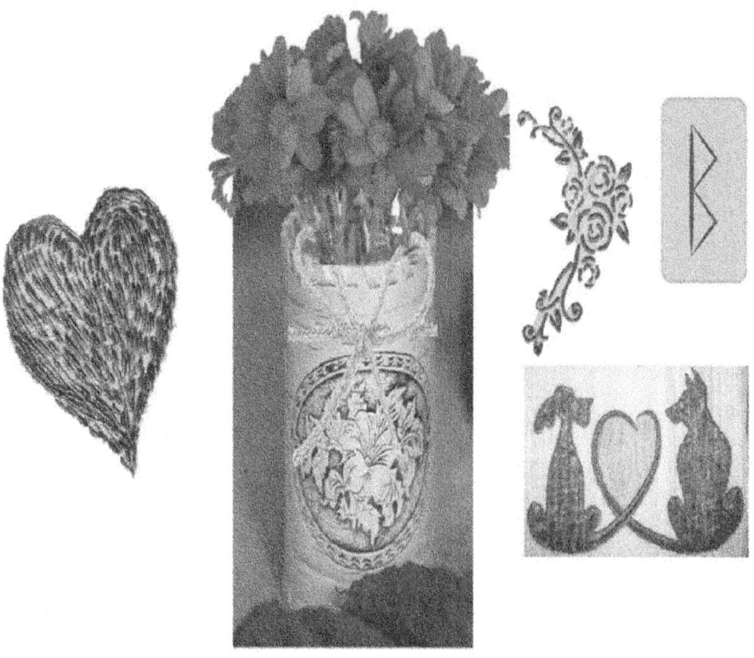

Flowers are a wonderful way to brighten up your home. That means that you will need a vase to accompany them. You can stop and grab flowers at any minimart or pick a bundle yourself and then put them in a beautiful wood burned vase that looks like you spent a bundle at a flower shop. Some flowers like potted orchids will bloom again in six months, so the lovely container will be used for a long time. Potted plants last much longer, or if you do not want to bother caring for flowers or a plant, you can always buy artificial silk flowers.

Materials

- Birch bark from any hobby or big box store

- Twine

- Tin cans

- Glue gun & sticks

- Wood burning kit

Steps

- Gather your tin cans and glue a birch strip around them. Make sure to glue at the beginning and at the end.

- Wrap some twine around the ends and tie in a bow because it adds an artistic look.

- Heat up your wood burner.

- With your pencil or any pattern you have printed (see suggestions illustrated below) you can draw any image, including a heart with someone's initials and an arrow.

- Trace over your design slowly and go over a few times.

- Fill in or shade with any of the techniques previously discussed.

Flower Arranging Tips

Start with the leaves and branches criss-crossing the stems. Cut your flowers in a way that the stems are not more than twice the height of your vase. Put the bigger flowers lower than the smaller ones. If there are roses, put the tallest ones in the center of the bouquet.

- Make a heart using your wood burning skills, attach it to a wooden skewer and stick it in the center of the bouquet (see image at top of the chapter).

Chapter 18:
Wood Burned Color Block Wall Art Quote

Everyone notices a good quote. They give us a quick burst of wisdom right when we need it. Offering an inspiration to start each day, especially when our normal "get-up-and-go" has lapsed can be very good for attaining a positive state of mind. There is actually a built-in bit of coaching benefit that happens to you when you read it.

Most people have heard old adages, you know, about smelling the roses. What that does is give us pause to remember to slow down, breathe, and live in the moment. In present times with everything being digital, a beautiful handcrafted quote is sure to spread happiness, joy or inspiration for anyone who looks at it.

Materials

- Tape (Painter's or Frog)

- Paint brush (foam)

- Wooden letters with paper template

- Acrylic paint

- Pencil

- Wood burning kit

- Pencil

- Poster strips

- Scissors

- Tape

Steps

- Lay your letters out so you can tell how the blocks of color work together.

- Begin by placing tape diagonally on the letters.

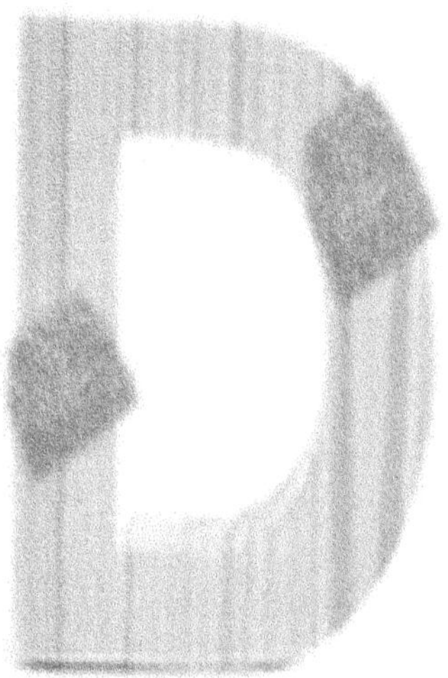

- Press the tape down firmly (the adhesive on the tape will be activated, stopping any seepage underneath from the paint).

- Using a foam paintbrush do the lower sections of each letter.

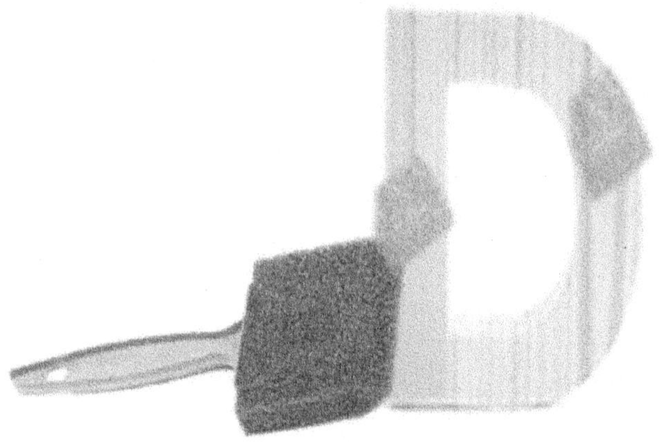

- Gently take the tape off after letting the paint slightly dry, being very careful not to get any of the wet paint from the tape on the wood that is unpainted (see picture below).

- With your pencil, sketch the pattern you imagined, for example, zig zags, stripes, stars, dots, you name it... on the top of each letter (see sample pattern illustration below).

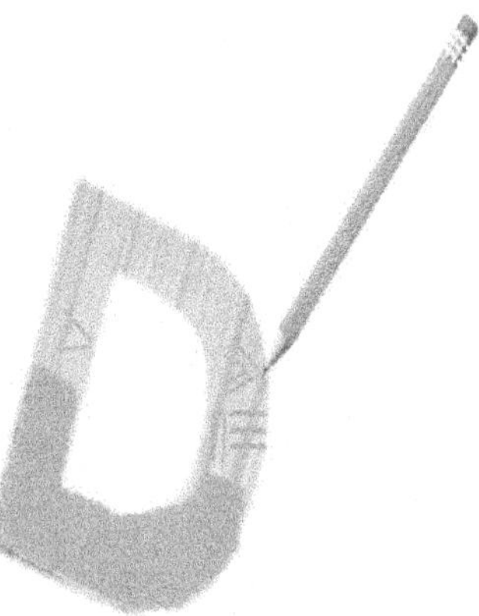

- Heat up your pyrography pen and begin going over the pencil lines. Erase any pencil lines that you did not completely cover.

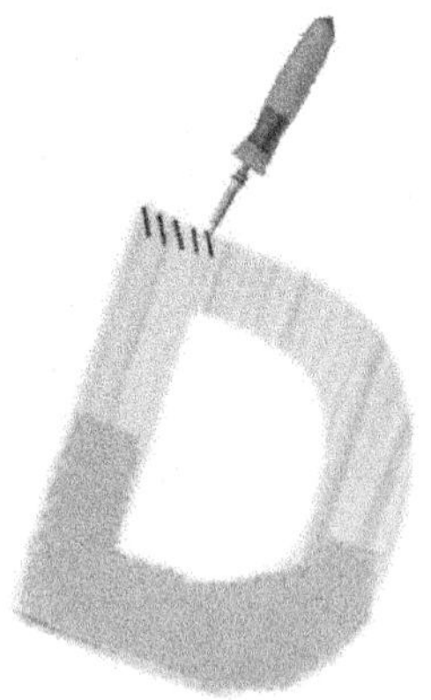

- Making sure it is level, tape your template to the wall. **Tip:** Cut your template in the way that you want your quote to be on the wall.

- After taping, gently trace the letter cutouts with a pencil.

- Place the adhesive poster strip on the back of your first letter and press it securely on the wall.

- Repeat Step 10 for all of the letters.

- Mount the quote on your wall! (See sample pattern below.)

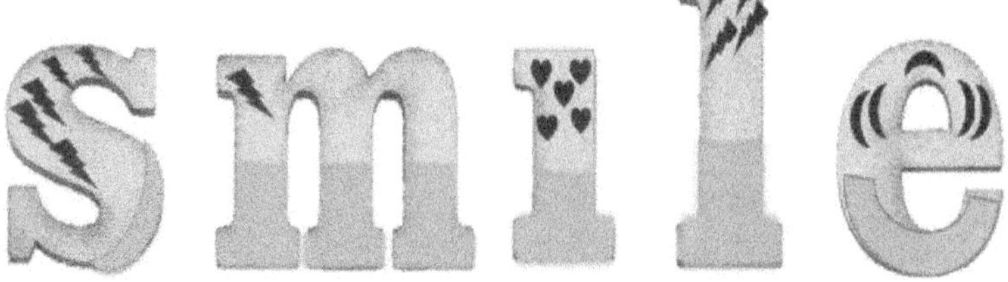

Chapter 19: Birthday Board

Paying homage to someone's birthday is a wonderful celebration and crafting a birthday board is a great way to show your loved ones how much you appreciate them. It is a celebration of how much the kids have grown over the past year. The board will make everyone whose name and birthday are burned into it feel special and they will literally see how much you love them. It can be really difficult trying to remember everyone's birthday. Having a birthday board will make life a bit easier...it's a notification! This birthday board will keep all of your family, friends and other significant people in your life in order, with their date literally burned in one place. You don't have to spend money on calendars or tape notes to your refrigerator to mark birthdays anymore. You don't have to count on someone whispering to you, "Hey tell Sally Happy Birthday!" You will know days, months, and even weeks ahead of time because it is hanging on the wall, beautiful and bold for everyone to see. It will also be a great gift for any occasion, so you may want to make a few of them.

Materials

- 6 inches x 8 inches pine board

- Table saw

- Needle-nose pliers.

- Wood burning kit

- Drill and ⅛ th drill bit

- 12 silver eye screws (small)

- 1½ inch wood disks (The number of disks should represent the number of people in your family with extras in case you need more for a gift or to add birthdays of others you want to celebrate, plus one never knows when a baby will be on board [pun intended]).

- 50 x 0.6 eyepins (long tails) twice the number of wood disks

- Small 0.5 per disc jump rings for linking them together. You can find jump rings and eye pins in any jewelry making section of a store.

Steps

- Saw the board to 26 inches in length using your table saw or hand saw.

  - **Here is a really cool trick:** On your computer pick your favorite font and enlarge it to the size you need for your sign. Make sure you make it the right length and width for your board. For this project it will say BIRTHDAYS (really big) (see examples below).

BIRTHDAYS

BIRTHDAYS

BIRTHDAYS

BIRTHDAYS

- Next, blow up your letters and crop them in parts that you can easily to put back together.

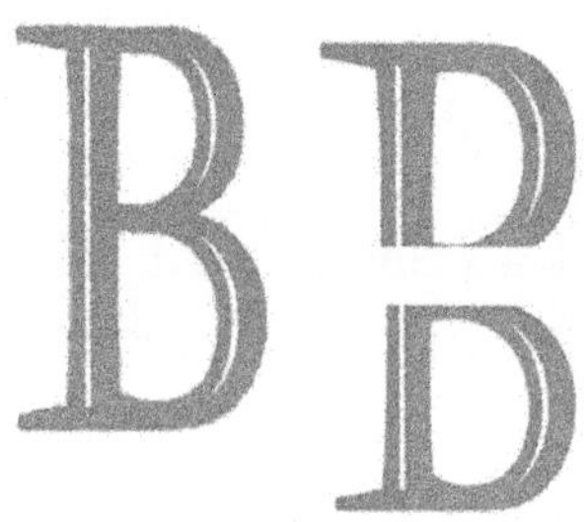

- Heat up your wood burner.

- Decide on a tip, either fine and rounded tip, calligraphy tip, very-fine sharpened tip, medium tip, or flat and fat tip. For this project the fine rounded tip and flat and fat tip are suggested.

- Burn the outline of your letters. Practice on a piece of scrap wood first until you decide on which of your new intermediate techniques you want to use. Watch out that on the curves you lean in the right direction.

- Using the fat and flat tip fill your letters.

- Print out or hand draw your small letters for the months of the year.

- Figure out your spacing. Subtract 1 ½ inches from the length of your board and then divide by twelve. That will give you the length you need between your screw eyes.

- Using a pencil on the narrow edge of the board draw a line to mark the middle of your month (such as, December - put the e over the line).

- For the month letters use your fine and rounded tip.

- Drill a very small hole in the center of each pencil line.

- Choose a stain to match your decor but do not go too dark.

- Apply your stain evenly and follow the wood grain.

- Wipe off excess stain with a lint-free cloth and let it dry.

- Give it plenty of time to cure. You may only need one coat.

- After your birthday board is completely dry, insert your screw eyes.

- Sort your circular wooden discs.

- Use a piece of scrap 2 x 4 (3 inches tall) to use as a drilling base and as a point for marking your holes. Also, get a pen.

- With a ruler mark a bisecting line in the circle at the middle. Make sure it is centered or the chains will hang crooked.

- With one of the extra discs, put it on the template you made from scrap wood and drill a hole in the top and one in the bottom using the middle line to show you where to drill. Be careful not to get too close to the edge.

- Now that you know where to drill, go to work on all of your discs.

- Now take the time to think about how you want to display each person's name and their birthday. Practice your best handwriting and burn the name and day on the front and the full birthday on the back (see image below).

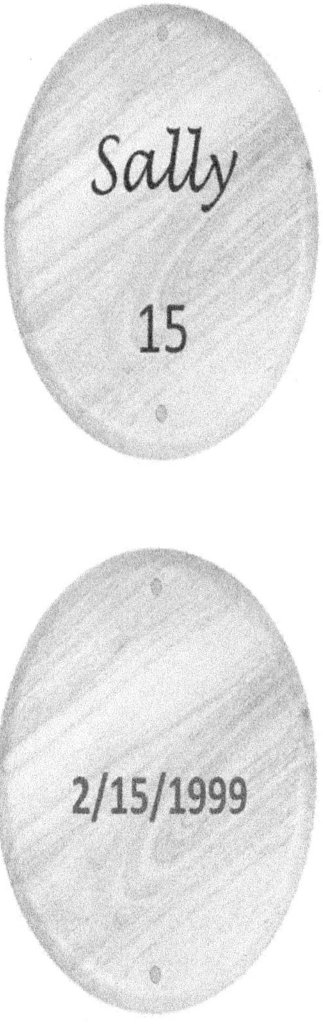

- Make sure you have everyone's birthday right!

- Feed the long end of your eye pins through one of the holes.

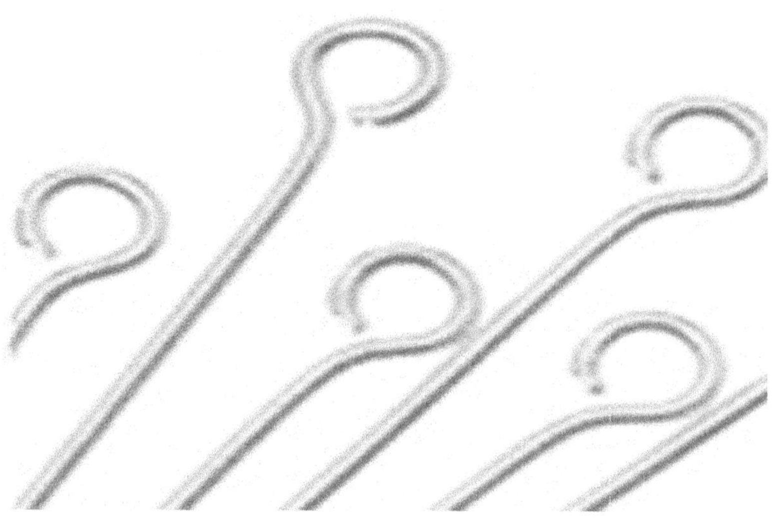

- Bend the tail and eye part up and toward the outer part of the circle with your needle-nose pliers.

- Using the pliers, twist the tail around the eye and pinch the wires together near the holes on the disc to stop them from wiggling.

- Guiding the tail, you can slide your pliers around in a circle and then just pinch and hide the end of the eye pins inside of the twists. Keep the eye parallel to the disc's flat side, that way they will be laying flat when you hand them up.

- Repeat Step 27 twice for each bottom and top hole on every disc (make a few blank ones since families do change and grow).

- Screw your screw eyes into the board under each of the months.

- Put your discs in piles by month, and then on those piles by the day.

- Connect each disc using a jump ring to link each disc to each other and to the board. Use the pliers to open up the eye rings and then pinch it closed again after you put on the jump ring. One jump ring goes in between two discs.

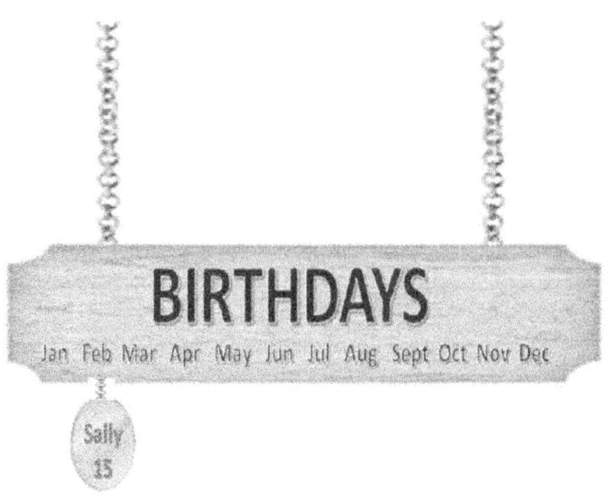

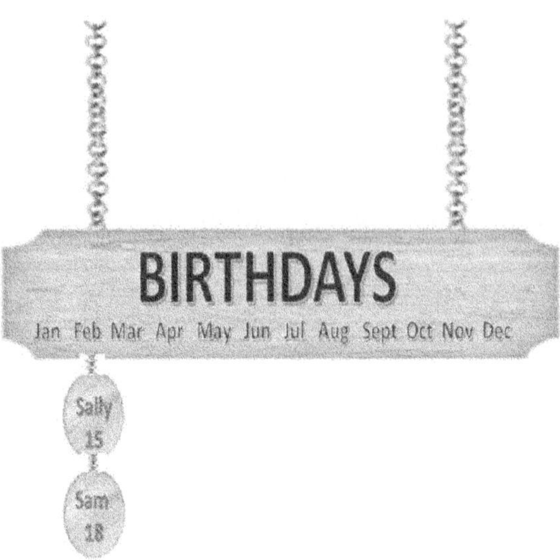

Tips For Success

- On your printer you will have a way to print a mirror image or backward image. This is called a transfer/iron on. Select the correct paper for your printer and your project.

- Cut wax paper the size of a sheet of paper and tape it to a thin card and feed it into the printer, and wowee you will have transferable letters that are soft and smudgeable! Be careful not to get it on your clothes or anything else.

- Very gently untape the wax from the card, flip it over and carefully set it ABOVE your board.

- Lay it flat, ink side down and rub the back with a spoon for a full minute and carefully lift off the wax paper.

Chapter 20: Ceremonial Mask Pyrography Project

Historically, in many cultures both ancient and modern, a ceremonial mask is for the purpose of a ritual or transformation. Ceremonial masks are still of monumental importance in some cultures today. They are beautiful and mystical and tell a story. Designing your own pattern is the way to go with this project because creative emotion should be the foundation for this type of wood burning creation. The mask for this project will be a conversation piece for the ages, as well as a compliment to your pyrography skill set. These ceremonial masks share many characteristics, and with highly detailed work, your project will appear magical and timeless. Masks are known to be mediators with the spirit world. Ritual and ceremonial masks are burned with hefty geometric line patterns and shapes that are abstract, as well as with designed facial features that show the emotion of a person.You can attach real animal fur, sea shells, or seed pods to enhance the human/animal impressions portrayed.

Materials

- Variable temperature burning unit

- Ball tip or looped tip pen

- Spear shader pen

- Curved shader pen

- 9 x 9 inch practice piece (poplar)

- 9 x 9 inch heart that is pre-cut

- Sandpaper (320-grit)

- Dry lint-free cloth

- Graphite paper

- #4 soft pencil

- Masking tape

- 8 inch square of brown paper (paper bag)

- Watercolor paints and watercolor pencils

- Ruler

- Polyurethane spray

Steps

- Definitely do some practice work.

- Find a pattern for your ceremonial mask

- Lightly sand your board with 320-grit in the direction of the wood grain and then get all the dust off with your dry cloth.

- Print the pattern of the mask you have chosen.

- Fold the pattern you printed in half (so the face centers match).

- Use your soft pencil and rub the back of your pattern leaving a dark coating of graphite.

- Using your ruler and a pencil, mark a vertical line in the center of your board.

- Set the centerfold of the paper with the pattern on it and mark a line on your board.

- Using tape attach the patterned paper one one side.

- Using your pen, trace the pattern's design, lifting a corner to make sure the whole design transferred.

- Remove the pattern and tape.

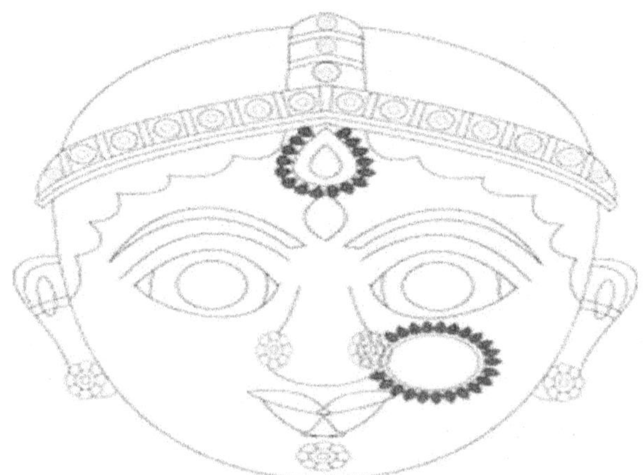

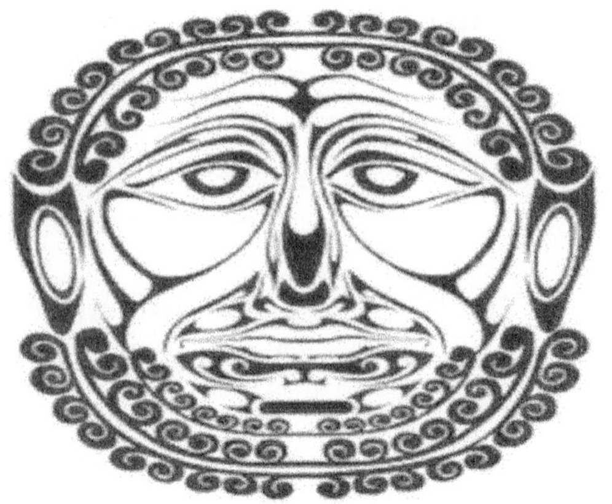

- Use your creativity to add feathering, beaded lines, or raffia strings.

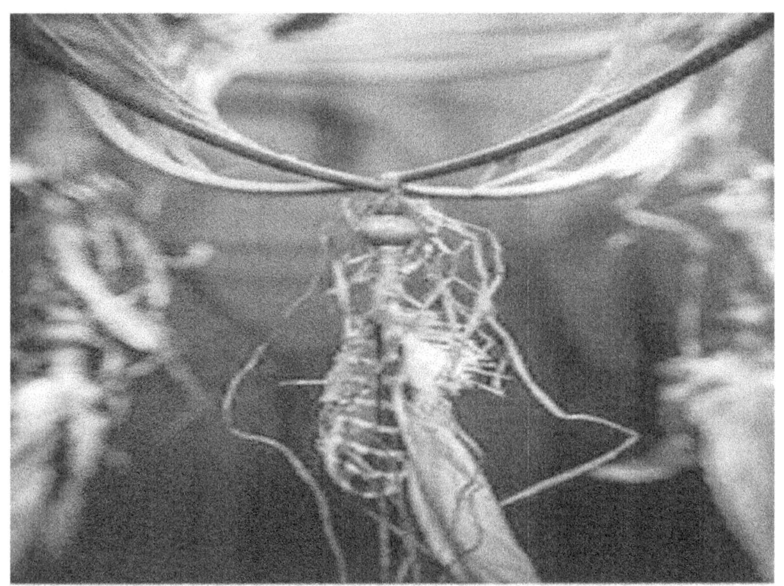
hutterstock.com • 1601866093

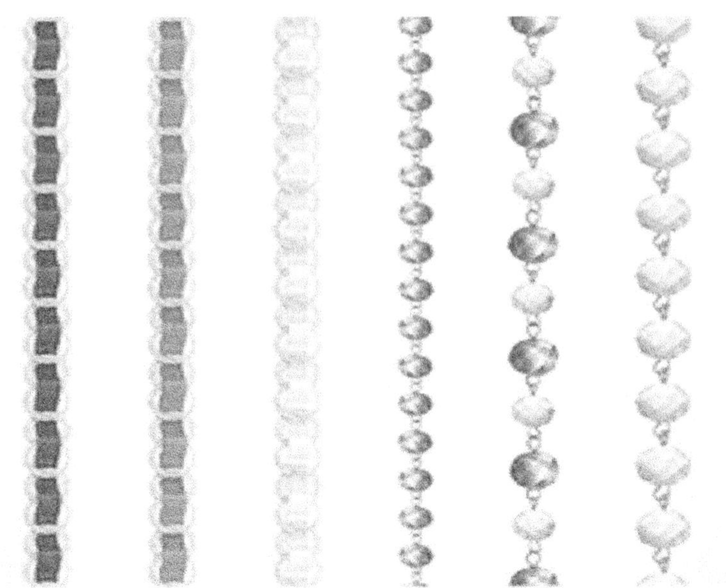
shutterstock.com • 299915234

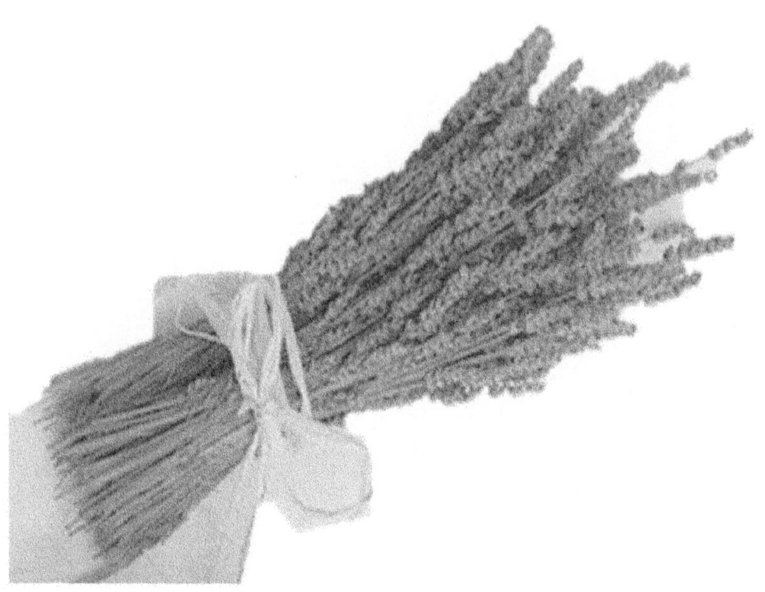

- With your spear shader, map your tonal area out with your pen on a low heat, using long pull strokes. Poplar is a very soft wood and dents quite easily, making it easy to work with.

- Along the raised areas of the face, use long pull strokes with your spear shader and shade around the top edges of the face lines according to your pattern. It is fun choosing a ceremonial face pattern. There are a few displayed for you below.

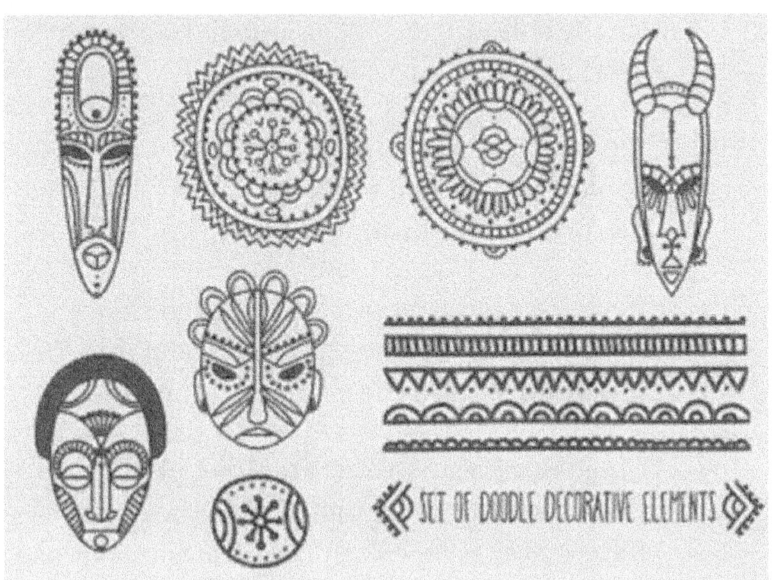

shutterstock.com • 347692388

- With the spear shader pen tip on the flat of the shader, and a #3 medium-pale tonal value setting, shade along the top right-hand sides of the raised elements in the face with long pull strokes.

- Use your creativity and the flat part of the spear shader to place highlights on the mask's nose ridge and cheek bones (medium temperature setting).

- Decorate the forehead since ceremonial masks usually have geometric decorations on the face, including the forehead.

- Use your looped or ball tip, and the dot technique you learned in previous chapters.

Use the solid fill dot technique to fill the eyes, nostrils, and mouth.

- Step back and look at the piece as a whole, you should see differing tonal areas from mid-tone dark brown to mid-tone light brown.

- Check for even, smooth and gradual shade work, making sure you have dark shading for the eyebrows, and the corners of the eyes.

- Using your spear shader and long pull stroke lines, create some feathers on the head (the image below is an example of feathers, but use whichever pattern you like the best).

- Start shading the center feather first at the edge, pulling toward the outer edge. Then start the next feather on the outer edge pulling toward the center of the feather. This technique creates a curved or rolled feathered impression.

- Make the background feathers a bit darker with long pull strokes giving a 3D look. It makes them look like they are tucked into each other.

- Using your looped tip pen, create six or seven layers of scrubbie strokes, tightly packed. See Chapter 2 to remind yourself how to do this. Do this over the feather's shaded areas to make it look even, gradual, and smooth.

- Work tightly packed thin lines into the side of each feather making them individual.

- Starting high and at the center of the shaft of the feather burn a gentle curve that drops down in the direction of the feather's outer edge.

- Thin, tightly packed lines are worked into the sides of the feathers to show the individual feather lines. Work each line in a gentle curve that starts high at the central feather shaft and drops down towards the outer edge of the feather (see example below).

- For the feather's veins use light pressure with your ball tip and quickly move your pen over

the wood. You can also use your spear shader
or your curve for fine, thin, lines.

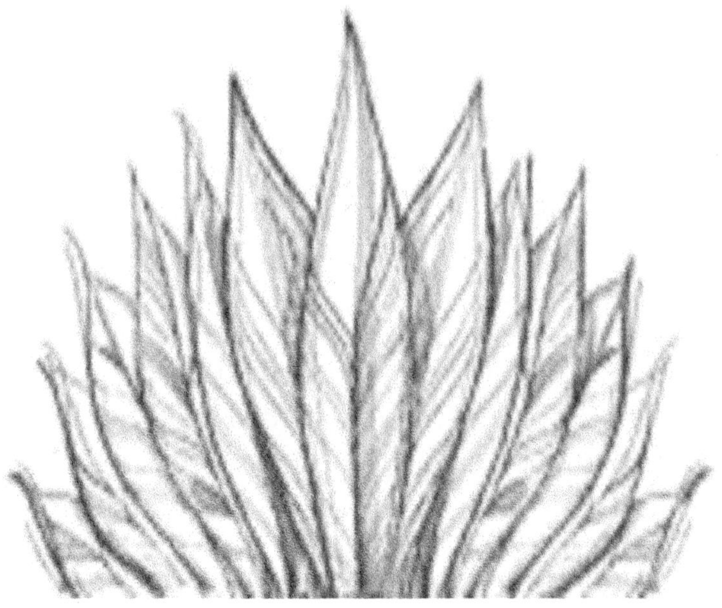

- Using your loop tip or ball tip to burn stripes,
  speckles, and spots onto your feathers.

- You can create stripes by using the slow motion
  and the long pulling line technique.

- Work right over the curved lines you shaded in
  the previous step. Moving the pen slowly will
  intensify the tonal value of the burn

- You can create speckles with the touch and lift
  dot technique you learned in Chapter 2. This
  leaves a medium size dark dot on your piece.
  Make the decorations on the feathers vary.

- Using your ball tip, shade in long straight hair (if you want hair) working from one of your decorations, such as beads or twine knots.

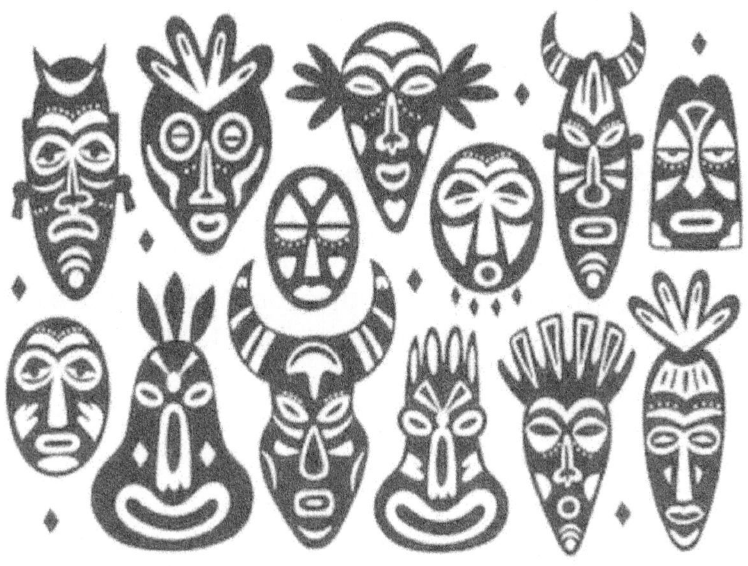

shutterstock.com • 1833182191

- Burn small s-shaped strokes along the twine to give the impression of twisted strings.

- By using high heat the grain of the wood will raise creating texture and dark tonal values.

- Take your brown paper and ball it up. Rub the balled-up paper over your burned design. It works like very fine sandpaper leaving no scratches or damage!

- Work the hair with basic shading in clumps. Then add individual strands of hair. (Note that you are moving along with the pattern of ceremonial mask print that you chose).

- The hair is worked in clumps for the basic shading, then individual hair strands are added. These next two steps are identical to the steps that created the feathers.

- Shade the clumps of hair with your spear shader using pull strokes on with a medium shade moving lighter. Burn closest to the face and outward toward the wood's edge (the same technique you used for the feathers).

- Set on a high temperature, using your looped tip or your curved shader, burn each individual line of hair.

- Use an eraser and remove any pencil marks (white artist eraser has no dye).

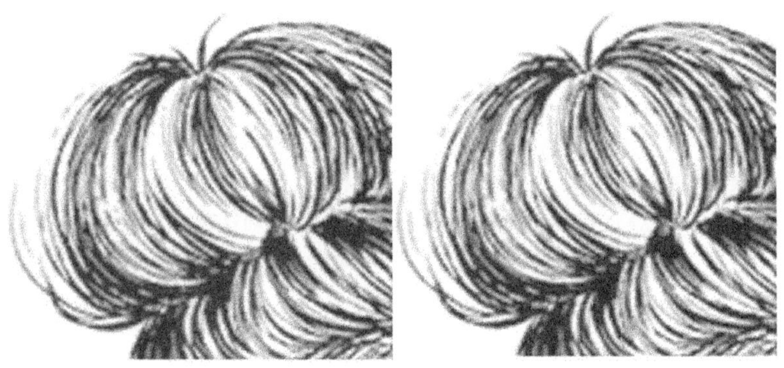

- Decide if you wish to add any color. If so, watercolor pencils and watercolor paint tint your wood without hurting your tonal value.

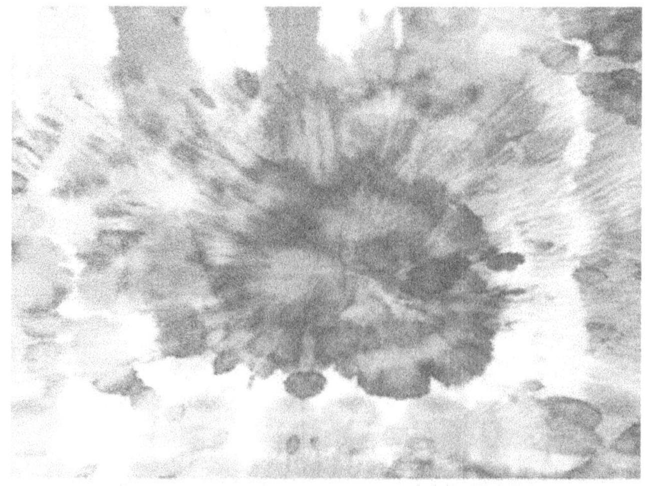

shutterstock.com • 1664543473

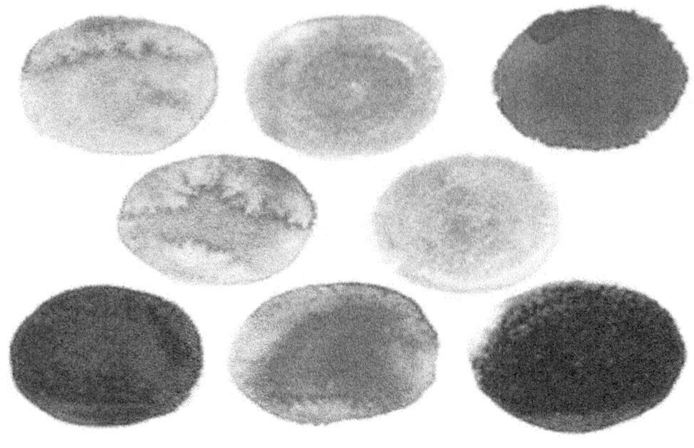

shutterstock.com • 163362863

- Ceremonial mask colors are usually in the black, brown, or rust hues (see example above), but you can always add color if that is what you imagined (see example below).

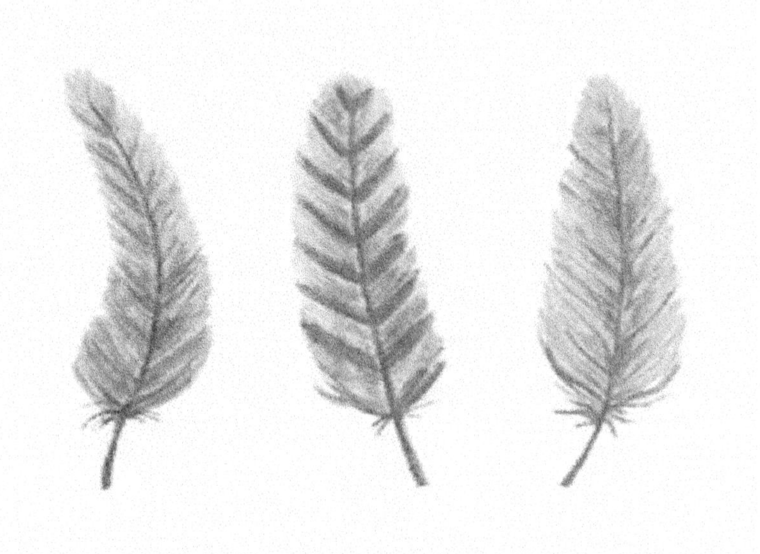

- Gently sand your piece again with your crumbled up ball of brown paper.

- Using your ball tip burner, sign and date your art including your city and your country.

- Following the directions on your spray sealer can, apply several coats, allowing them to dry in between.

Chapter 21: Baby Crib Mobile

You can just about imagine a project for every room in your house, but the baby's room is a whole different ball game. A mobile for baby is way more than just an adorable toy. It can help to calm and soothe the baby as well as stimulate the little one's brain. Sensory stimulation is important for the developing brain and that is where your mobile comes in. Just imagine when that little one grows up and has their own little ones, being able to pass down a handcrafted wood burned baby mobile. One of the main functions of a baby mobile is to visually stimulate the baby's growth because their vision is still developing (Babymobile.com, 2020). Mobiles also help in the development of motor skills because the baby will try to follow the moving parts. That is why this project has vertically and horizontally moving pieces.

Materials

- Pine skirting board, measuring 4 x 47 x 10 millimeters

- 3 wooden dowels, measuring 20 x 10 millimeters

- Power drill

- Wood drill, 3 millimeters

- Hole saw, 75 millimeters

- Transparent elastic

- Hand vice

- Scrap wood

Steps

- Using your vice firmly hold down the dowel against a piece of scrap wood to prevent it from splitting during the drilling procedure.

- Mark in pencil three holes on each piece of dowel and then drill them.

- Using the hole saw on your power drill, make a circle shape so the hole saw makes a big hole in the middle of the circle. By doing it on scrap wood you can use the circle as a template.

- Retract the bit on your drill from the center of the saw so the rest of the discs you make do not have a drill hole.

- With your vice, secure the scrap wood template onto a wooden skirting board.

- Cut out your discs. The template will prevent the hole saw from sliding.

- Cut out nine discs from the skirting board.
  ***Note: if you do not have a hole saw, cut the
  discs with a jig saw or buy them pre-made.

- Drill holes in the center of five of the discs and
  next, drill holes through the diameter of the
  remaining four discs (this is where you will
  thread the discs).

- Heat up your wood burner.

- Customize your design with creativity. Here are
  some examples:

  - stars

  - moons

  - letters

  - numbers

  - smiley faces

- Stain the discs and let dry.

- Thread the piece of elastic through the center
  holes you drilled on the dowels. Alternate with
  a disc.

- Measure a piece of elastic to around 5 feet (this
  can be trimmed later).

- Tie several knots on one end and then thred one of the discs so it is hanging vertically.

- Tie a knot at the bottom of the disc.

- Leaving a one inch gap tie five or six more knots and then thread a disc through the center hole. Repeat the process changing the discs from hanging vertically to horizontally (see image below).

- Leave the extra elastic for when you get to the top for hanging the mobile later.

- Once you have the center column threaded, hang discs on each of the ends. (Note: The end discs are individually tied so that the mobile will rotate and cast shadows for the baby's enjoyment.)

- Tie the discs to the end holes of the dowel and tie a few knots to secure the discs.

- Hang the mobile by attaching it to a ceiling hook and then watch the baby wonder at your craft.

Chapter 22:
Pyrography Long Shoe Horn

The shoe horn got its name because centuries ago they were made from animal horns. Some still are today. Elizabeth I had her blacksmith make her one so she wouldn't strain her back (BestShoesStretchers.com, 2020). Many people have a history of back problems and one item that can help tremendously is a long handled shoe horn. Shoes are one of our basic necessities for everyday life. With or without age it can become irritating and even painful trying to get shoes on, especially if they are tight. It is much easier to use a wooden shoe horn than one of those metal ones. The image below is a sample of a woodburned long shoe horn for a Grandpa. Imagine the happiness of Grandpa not having to bend over anymore, and also seeing a handcrafted personalized wooden shoe horn made especially with him and his comfort in mind. That shows love.

Everyday of sticking your thumb in the back of your shoes to slip them on destroys the shoe's heel counter. Plus, it ruins the way the shoe looks and it can hurt your hands. This handcrafted long shoe horn will extend the life of your shoes. This is something to keep in mind when shoes are expensive. This proves to be highly beneficial for people who have back problems. If you have back problems, you cannot afford to take chances. Thus, the long handle makes it a lot easier for people such as them to just hold the handle and place their feet inside those shoes nicely and quickly.

This long shoe horn will work perfectly especially if Grandpa wears boots. Boot coverings are long over the calves and therefore, only a really long shoe horn will work. So make the length of your shoe horn handle more than the length of the boots.

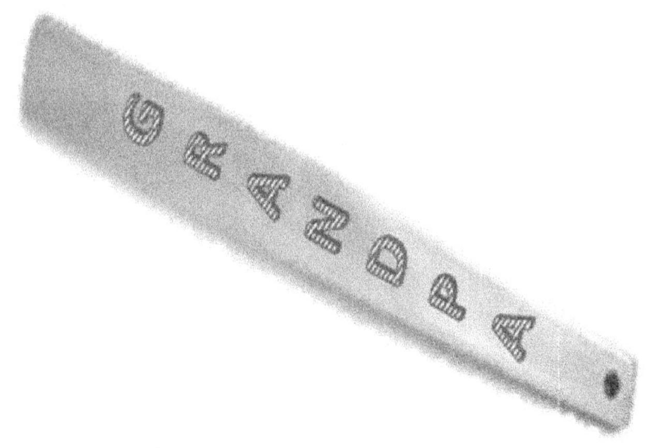

Materials

- One 20 inch long by 3 inches wide and ¾ inch thick wooden plank (or longer is the person you are crafting for is very tall). Use hardwood such as oak, maple, walnut, or cherry because

the tip will be sanded thin for grasping and
softer wood may crack.

- Belt sander

- Band saw

Steps

- Sketch a ten inches long shape so that it can
  taper into a thin tip to easily insert into a shoe
  by making the sides symmetrical.

- With your belt sander, using a coarse-grit, sand
  out a flute.

- Work using the nose slowly and gradually back
  and forth across the length. (Note: If you do
  not have a belt sander, make it a project to
  sand and sand making the flute smooth.)

- Taper the thickness down to $\frac{1}{8}$ of an inch at
  the tip of the shoe horn.

- Once you are at $\frac{1}{8}$ of an inch keep sanding with
  120-grit until all of the grooves are out.

- Using a jar trace a semi-circle on the tip of your
  shoe horn.

- Draw the side profile tapering your lines
  toward the tip of the shoe horn.

- Taper the handle toward the other end.

- Cut the side profile.

- Smooth the line transitions leaving about 1/16 of an inch of wood outside of the line for you to sand later.

- Using tape adhere the cut off piece back onto the shoe horn so your surface is stable for cutting.

- With your band saw cut the top profile.

- Again, leaving a small amount of wood outside of the line, cut around the circumference.

- Drill a hole on the tip of the shoe horn so it can hang by the closet.

- Taper the tip to a smooth and rounded gentle surface with sandpaper or a sander.

- Heat up your wood burning kit and GET CREATIVE!

- Apply your polyurethane finish because it is non-abrasive for the beating it will take over the years.

- With this new and personalized handcrafted long handled shoe horn there will be no need to bend when putting on shoes again!

Chapter 23: Moving on to the Advanced Level of Wood Burning

Hopefully, you have thoroughly enjoyed crafting all of the projects and improving your skills in Circular Motion Shading, Uniform Strokes, Pulling Motion Shading, Dot Motion Shading, Zig Zag Motion Shading, Side Shading, Line Shading, and Texturing.

Now you have learned that using a wide and flat tip for shading, such as your curved edge or spear shader is one of your best techniques. You have practiced plenty now with your pull motions and various other techniques. The wood burning art projects and techniques have been fully detailed in this guide for intermediate wood burning. Details about temperature setting, textured patterns, layering, and the speed of a stroke, along with finishing techniques have now prepared you at a more advanced skill level and your practice has given you lots of confidence.

In this book you learned how to recognize visual tones as dark and light values. With best intentions, you confidently realized your artful potential and learned how to relax while you were burning. You now know new skills and techniques for using various tools, and gained more insight into wood burning as a form of art. You have learned how to express your ideas more creatively. Learning the characteristics of the wood that is used and how to add to the ambiance of your home or workplace is an amazing skill that will impress others. Now you realize the natural markings such as rings and grain flow make each project different from the next.

Become familiar with The Walnut Hollow Versa Tool and the Razertip Pyrographic, as well as the Utility Wood Burner. These are great tools. Learning how to add color and taper table legs are advanced wood burning skills. The fire epoxy table is a special project that moves you into the advanced level of pyrography. When people see your handcrafted welcome sign it will let them know they are at a crafter's home. Surely, you enjoyed burning your favorite superhero portrait and maybe you gave it as a gift.

This book was full of perfect handcrafted gifts for any occasion, and best of all they are all one-of-a-kind. Now that you have the skill and all of the tools in your burner kit, go out and use them!

Now that you have finished reading this book, you're probably wondering, "What do I do next?" Your head is probably spinning with new ideas, measuring where you are in your pyrography journey, trying to figure out what project you want to apply your new skills to. This doesn't mean you are finished learning, the more experience you have with pyrography, the better prepared you will be for expert level crafting.

References

Baby Mobile.com. "Benefits of Infant Mobiles".
     Babymobile.com, 2020.
     http://www.babymobile.com/benefits-of-
     infant-mobiles

Best Shoes Stretchers.com. "Shoe Horn for Boots and
     its Advantages". Best Boots and Shoe Care
     Wares. 2020
     https://www.bestshoesstretchers.com/shoe-
     horns-for-boots/

Clark, Matt. "Safety and Health Concerns with
     Pyrography" Pyrography World 8/16/2016.
     http://pyrographyworld.com/index.php/2016/
     08/16/safety-and-health-concerns-with-pyr
     HYPERLINK
     "http://pyrographyworld.com/index.php/2016
     /08/16/safety-and-health-concerns-with-
     pyrography/"ography/

Lowes Editorial Team. "Wood-Burning Basics".
     Lowes.com, 2020.
     https://www.lowes.com/n/ideas-
     inspiration/woodburning-basics

Pyrocrafters. "Best Woods for Burning" Pyrography,
     2020.
     https://www.pyrocrafters.com/best-woods-
     for-wood-burning/

Sun Catcher Studio. Pyrography – Wood burning Tips and Tools. Sun Catcher Studio, 2020. https://suncatcherstudio.com/

The Pyrography Tool. "Tips and Tricks" 2020 http://www.thepyrographytool.com/wood-burning-tips-and-tricks/

Walnut Hollow. "Special Technique Points." 3/07/2020. https://www.walnuthollow.com/assets/3/7/Tutorial-sm33all.pdf

Wengert, G. "Southern Yellow Pine: Why Some People Prefer Spruce". Woodworking Network, 2016. https://www.woodworkingnetwork.com/wood/wood-month/southern-yellow-pine-why-some-people-prefer-spruce

Working the Flame.com. "A Brief History of Pyrography Art & Wood Burning [Updated]." Working the Flame, 2020. https://workingtheflame.com/history-of-pyrography/

Ak NO, Cliver DO, Kaspar CW. Cutting Boards of Plastic and Wood Contaminated Experimentally with Bacteria. J Food Prot. 1994 Jan;57(1):16-22. doi: 10.4315/0362-028X-57.1.16. PMID: 31113021.

Printed by BoD™ in Norderstedt, Germany